MARY B. GALLWEY

Gotham Books

30 N Gould St.
Ste. 20820, Sheridan, WY 82801
https://gothambooksinc.com/

Phone: 1 (307) 464-7800

© 2023 *Mary Gallwey*. All rights reserved.

No part of this book may be reproduced, stored in a retrieval system, or transmitted by any means without the written permission of the author.

Published by Gotham Books (November 28, 2023)

ISBN: 979-8-88775-558-8 (P)
ISBN: 979-8-88775-559-5 (E)

Because of the dynamic nature of the Internet, any web addresses or links contained in this book may have changed since publication and may no longer be valid.

The views expressed in this work are solely those of the author and do not necessarily reflect the views of the publisher, and the publisher hereby disclaims any responsibility for them.

Contents

Preface v

Part One 1

Part Two 96

Part Three 149

Preface

Along the way of each soul's journey, answers come—promptings, words of understanding and compassion—to the one reaching for the wisdom of the ages. Help for the one who asks, who strives for direction, comes unfailingly in many forms. Universal knowing is expressed in the language it can best be understood by the receiver, working its way through a myriad of beliefs, cultural understandings, and traditions. Yet they come from and lead to the oneness of existence, whatever name we give to that.

There is a voice in this book that is addressing the author, and hence perhaps the reader. These words came to me at unexpected times, often in times of struggle, sometimes in times of new insights, over the course of the last several years. I recognize the source but have no name for it—just a flow of words that cause a quick grab for paper.

Each piece in this book stands alone. Some may enjoy opening the book randomly to see what they find of particular relevance. I recommend reading only one or two at a time so allow space to contemplate.

Although the words seemed very personal when I wrote them down, they also felt universal. I have shared some of these messages with others who have commented that they were just what they needed to hear at the time. So, I decided to make them available in the hope they will be of help to others in making their own individual connection with their own source of wisdom.

M. B. G

Part One

Author's Note:

I am the one being spoken to throughout this book, and the words in plain text reflect what I have heard. My words, primarily in Part two, are in italics. M.B.G (See Preface)

Along this path of life there are steps to take, but they are not in a linear progression as you might see it. You imagine looking upward, but that which you are seeking is everywhere. The process is one of letting it in, pulling at the door until it opens. You struggle to understand, but your brain cannot. It is your spirit that can respond as you allow that essential one that you are to manifest. It is a matter of allowing rather than achieving.

You walk through this life through a mixture of darkness and light intertwined, each pulling toward different ends. As you choose your direction, ask to find the wisdom to fulfill what you are here to do.

Embrace with a free and open heart all that is being offered to you. As your trust erases resistance, the gifts flow freely where they are meant to go and do what they are meant to do in an ordered way.

However, it may look, all is well. Fix your attention on the place where perfection reigns, where the war has been won, where the light is eternally glorious, and love is the power that permeates and unites, gathers in, and expands.

While you are being cared for so immaculately, you have the opportunity to care for others. Learn how to do that from your heart, with the clarity of the view you are given when you melt into the feeling of the presence. Discover it. Savor it. See with new eyes and beware of old habits, assumptions, reactions. Only the wisdom gained along the way applies. Hold on to the driving constants within you, for they have led you faithfully.

*B*y the limitations of their essential human nature, human beings cannot comprehend the nature of that which many call god. They anthropomorphize it, projecting onto the infinite their own mental constructs, their own emotions, even their own shortcomings. That being does not think human thoughts, does not have human emotions, and certainly does not have human shortcomings.

So, what is a poor human to do? What human beings have been gifted with is the capacity to feel the presence, to experience that unnamable essence that can flow through to them, and which is so eminently attractive.

The omniscient mind of the source of all encompasses what you cannot know as a single being within a small circle in current time, a miniscule dot in the infinite stream. How do you even know what to ask for? Or what would be best? That's not to say that you should have no wants but try to acknowledge your limitations and trust the irrefutable knowing that comes from your higher self, your place of connection with all that emanates from your source.

As you recognize your essential ignorance, even in the midst of all your plans and aims, you open a door of possibility—a new way of seeing, a new kind of knowing.

There is no reason to shut out your wants or to cover them up. Simply open yourself to the larger picture, the amazing panorama of possibilities that lay before you as you welcome the guiding hand that is so kindly offered—ready like any good parent to scoop you up before you fall, inspire alternative choices, light the fire of love in your heart, urge you gently on in sync with your long-term journey.

You learn these things from your own experience and through the teaching of those who inspire you. You are given metaphors and similes to help you relate to the infinite, to help your mind construct the scaffolding for the building of your understanding. They are fine, but they do not define. Over time, you must learn to quiet your mind so that experience beyond words can take you into the boundless realms where you absorb enlightenment by opening yourself to it.

From experiences like that comes the ultimate knowing that each one must find individually as the unique one they are. This is the birthplace of wisdom—so different from even the most elaborate brain-based understanding. This is the gift to the one who reaches out in trust and longing.

*A*ccept the gifts your own life affords you. The gifts of others will not fit. Most likely you do not yet know all that you are, for the life ahead of you is still there to discover it.

Surrender your imaginings to the gift of the moment and watch the sun emerge from the clouds. Bask in its light; relax in its warmth; be renewed by its rays again and again. Instead of seeking what isn't, embrace what is, and the light of the eternal sun will shine through you whether you are aware of it or not.

There is nothing to fear. Just let yourself be filled in the way that is unique to you. It is neither better nor worse than what happens for another. It is your own path. Let your effort be to stay on it.

Those tugs of discomfort that you feel inside are your ties to the many things you have assigned importance to. In the larger perspective, only one thing matters—syncing up with and joining the oneness of that which all are a part. Everything else derives its importance from that, in relationship to that. If you are seated in that experience with the strength of your will and the clarity of your choice, you will know what and how anything else matters or does not.

You are living in the world of between, where opposing forces meet. The "under miners" come in a vast array of forms—random thoughts and feelings, negative emotions, threatening situations. Each one issues you a personal invitation to turn away from your knowing and attend to them instead.

There are three responses. The first is not a response, actually. It is maintaining your place of connection, a place from which you can observe with insight rather than entanglement. You can speak or act, if need be, with impunity. You can, perhaps, be useful. The second response is one of quick recognition that you have entered into the negative consciousness of whatever it is, and that prompts you to turn back to your knowing. The third one is entanglement, and that is much harder to get free from.

Ordinary life gives you repeated chances to practice this business of learning to hold on to the clarity that emanates from deep acceptance of your essential well-being. The more frequently you recognize when you have veered off from that knowing and turn back, the longer you will be able to maintain the state of balance from which you can make clear choices.

See it. See what is happening: the ongoing choices, the ongoing realignment, clearing the way to the deeper joy of letting go to the power that waits to fill the emptiness. The more you feel that the less you will tolerate being drawn away.

There are times when your effort is small, yet your longing opens the door. Your openness to what is offered to you, your mere confirmation of what you want, is enough for you to receive an abundance of love that is beyond what you have ever known.

You are accustomed to identifying the darkness, to cringing at the negative that you see and feel in your world. Make a shift. See the beauty, the good, the miracles that abound unnoticed. You have little idea of the power of that or of the power of THAT which you cannot name.

When you identify what is wrong in this world, be objective about it. Stay disconnected from it. Let it be your signal to reinforce your connection with the eternal good that it may flow through you. This is so very important. Above all, this is your work—to see the good, to focus on the good.

This is not to say that you should be naïve. To the contrary, you need to be wise enough to be alert to the subtle things that eat away at your strength.

Appreciate the gift that keeps on giving. When you see rocks in the waters surrounding your ship, know that those are also a gift. See them, even learn from them, and then turn away. Steer toward your safety. It comes not from rock-free waters but from your developing connection to your higher self. You can trust that no matter what happens.

Think of your life's circumstances as being a training ground for reaching your ultimate goal. As you line up your attention and energy with that goal, your way of seeing, understanding, and interacting with these "circumstances" changes. Circum means "around." Stare means "stand." Circumstance refers to all that "stands around" you.

How they are in the sense of "good" and "bad" depends hugely upon how you interface with them, how you see them. Are they to be like weights in a gym that you employ in successive degrees to build the strength you need to move toward your goal? Or are they obstacles in your way to a perceived state of more immediate enjoyment, safety, or satisfaction?

You, like most, get caught in reactivity to the immediate, often with knee-jerk responses to circumstances. Yet you possess the ability to choose the "road less traveled," the one that leads to the long-term goal. The strength to build is one of focused energy, and it emerges out of discipline, effort, and practice.

That strength gives your intention the energy it needs to escape the resistance embedded in your very being. As you use and develop it, you are infused with both immediate delight and the privilege of being part of the thrust of evolution, the potential destiny of humanity.

It is no less than the magic of transformation that you experience as you develop mastery—consistency of intention, clarity of desire, power of will, and the utter freedom of one who serves.

Along the Way

Choose your way of seeing repeatedly. As you do, you are infused with the unified energy of others moving in the same direction.

Though alone in your choice, you are never alone. Enjoy the ongoing rearrangement of the furniture of your life. Look for the flow of the energy that comes and flow along with it.

Listening is the topic for today. It is a skill developed through practice and attraction to the wisdom that waits to manifest within you for the signal of your desire for it.

Think of the attention that a new love receives. That is how it is when the feeling flows. It is natural, and, beyond that, it is meticulously personalized for you. A perfect fit. Ask for the gift of hearing, of being taught, and ask for the gift of understanding. Each experience of that emanates from the unending source of all calling you back to itself.

So how does one stay tuned to that which you think will take you away while you walk upon the ground through your daily life? How do you do that? Listen and heed. For this is the essence of learning for you that can only take place exactly where you are. There is no place where the infinite cannot go with you, no space within you it cannot fill.

It doesn't have to take you away. The work is here. Go together.

By listening, you will learn to make the essential distinctions between what is based in truth and what is based in illusion, between what would lure you into its lair of destruction and what offers to lead you to joy. When it is suggested that you learn to listen, it is not only to words or sounds coming your way. An even better way of saying it would be, "Stay tuned."

All plans that you make so diligently can be rendered irrelevant in the blink of an eye. That doesn't mean not to make them. What it means is not to become so attached to them that you don't even notice when the situation changes.

Be ready for anything. There is only one constant, and amazingly enough, that one constant energizes continual motion. Are you ready to move with it? To change direction seamlessly? To do that, you have to stay in listening mode.

That is challenging for you because you like to feel you have some control over things. And you do. What you need to understand is what you have control over and what you do not. You decide or choose your intentions. You navigate your way as best you can toward a goal or goals that you can choose for yourself. And all of that is both huge and minute.

There is a naturalness to living in the moment. It is not as you imagine. Go ahead with your schedules, lists, plans. Just be ready to let go of them and turn your direction quickly. If you set the grand goal, then you can allow that to be your navigator.

Maintaining a consciousness illuminated by the very presence of infinite being is the pathway to attaining unity with it. Good and bad for you at any moment is determined more by what keeps you in that consciousness or takes you away from it. That's what so many forget.

It is not particular actions in themselves that take you away but your own wandering into the world of confusion and delusion that undermines your intent. The same path that takes you to unity leads to chaos when you turn your back in retreat.

The pathway is given to you, and you have glimpsed where it leads. The way is lit partly by the light of your own desire. Let it shine forth. Come with the truth of your own sincerity, and all else will be given.

Grant to your longing the strength of your will. Ask for direction, and it will come to you in many forms. Be alert, for your purpose is singular. It is one. See the one in the many, and you will begin to understand. Effort is rewarded and need not be strained.

There is but one way for you and only you can walk it. That is the way you must find. Each unique being has their own path, though all paths lead toward the same goal. Longing and will. They are your direction finders.

Love and strength. Heart and courage. And from that which is infinite, love and light. These primal elements have their seat within you, waiting to be your resources in all circumstances, at all times. Turn to them and behold the unfolding gift. Set no limits, for as the giver becomes your resource, you may become a resource of the giver. And that is a source of great joy. Hold on and let go. Got it? They actually go together.

Many of the thoughts that lead you astray are none of your business, plain and simple. They have the quality of stickiness that grabs your attention, which allows them to grow. What you focus on multiplies.

This is not easy stuff, especially as you become more aware of the little things that drain you. It is only your attraction to your higher self that can pull you away, protect you. Tend to that. It is the deep-rooted tree you can hold onto during a hurricane or the milder and harder-to-recognize spins.

You are exposed to things every day that pull at you like wind. You also have a tree to hold onto when the wind is strong, its trunk reaching upward to show you how to stay protected and separate.

Decision and division. Your decision is what puts the division between you and the stickiness. So, you have to recognize the need for it as soon as you feel the first pull or even before. Sometimes you must be ruthless about it. Always, you need to be firm. Be on the lookout; forewarning is a blessing.

The light shines within you, an eternal flame. The fuel for your experience of it is your attention. The light will not go out, but it can become distant for you, almost inaccessible. Recognize your need, connect to your longing, and add the logs of your focused attention to the fire.

Receive not just the comfort of the roaring flame keeping the wolves at bay, but let it shine through you to wherever it needs to go. That is your frontier, the edge of where you are. This energy does not need your directives, for it has its own. It can be polite in that it waits for your permission so you can join in. Time is short; the universe is vast; each moment is important.

It is time to establish a new normal in your life, where what has been an occasional blessing of feeling the presence of the eternal becomes the pervasive state. This presence awakens the dormant consciousness of all your sentient cells and expands outward. Its essence is radiance of a kind that moves through and out, through and out. The out is important. Without the air of that, it is stifled.

Welcome it, seek it out, and let it roam freely until it is your normal and any movement away from it stands out starkly, demanding your attention. It is actually always there, this radiant presence, but as powerful as it is, it awaits your welcome. It behaves as a guest in the very house it gave to you, for it seeks the unification of intentions.

No need to try to understand these words with your brain. The way to understanding is through absorbing the presence and letting it shine through you. That happens so naturally when you simply stay with it. Become the guest of your guest, the servant of the one who comes to your aid, the witness of the unfolding.

This is your shelter from the muck that abounds in the world you live in. This presence within you touches and then multiplies the presence in others—mostly without you awareness—and forms a vast web of strength and connection among awakened souls.

The newness of each moment is hidden by the seamless way it flows from the previous moment to the next. Adding to that, we tend to carry the load of past moments or even large clusters of them along with us to the extent that the newness is easily missed. We ourselves change as time streams by, but do we see that change? Are we present enough to notice? To appreciate it?

A survival skill of the human species is to keep looking forward in anticipation of what might happen on the road ahead. We look for the panther that might be hiding in the bushes and project our thoughts toward readiness for defense. This skill has its value, but it also pulls us away from what is really happening as opposed to what might.

The opportunity lies in awareness, consciousness of the newness that can free one from the bindings of the past. Awareness offers the possibility of freedom from conditioning and the gift of seeing the familiar freshly.

Boredom fades and the routine can be seen as new and even unpredictable, the mundane enjoyable.

It can be disturbing to be unable to look far into the future and predict the turns in life. The fact is that we cannot predict how even the most carefully planned future will turn out. Planning is fine as long as we remember that.

Life is for the living and "living" implies more than continued breath.

It means being there for all that is, absorbing the joy of simply being alive, of the freshness of moments attended to. Should real danger occur, the habit of being aware supports a readiness for self-protection and that of others. Try it out in short spans of time and learn, freshly. You will be amazed.

Whatever the intention, the essential self of each one is constantly changing. The person you will be at the time of anticipating an event is not the same as the one you will be should it happen, nor will it be exactly as you expected.

Presence in the present is the present. And the present is the ability to experience the constant presence of spirit, our own or that of the larger form of existence in its purest state, its eternal state.

The baby of the being lies within you at your very core. It needs nurturing, attention, and the freedom to grow. Cradle it and shower it with the truest love you can. Its cries are to be heeded at all costs. Its smiles delight you for they are of light as the word implies.

You do not need to understand to respond. What you need is to recognize. It is not your persona that has this eternal calling. It is the essence of you that seeks manifestation, that is a part of the overall unfolding of creation.

Here is the truth of it. There was a time when this essence of you entered the body of the child born to your mother. That child took its first of the stream of breaths that will define the span of its life on earth. The infinite has come to roost in the finite where creation is still happening.

Along the Way

What do you want to grasp hold of on this particular journey? The eternal essence that seeks to fulfill its mission or the particulars of this finite story of your current life?

Nourish the babe. Allow it to grow. Let it choose its destiny. Host its presence in this world of time.

You are endowed with life that is inherently eternal, and that life is expressing itself in the body of a person who lives in a place, interacts with other people, moves through places, and is affected by situations and conditions.

This person has all manner of things going on, some enjoyable, some enriching, some challenging, some threatening or problematic. And this person lives a life that is limited in time. In that limited time, you have the opportunity to bring the wisdom and purpose of the eternal into all the aspects of the life you are living. Learn to give that precedence above everything else.

When you do that as the very person you are, you become part of creation itself. You experience all the pulls, the puzzles, and the predicaments; and you experience the desires, the hopes, and the dreams. And with all of that, you make your choices. Place your well-being in the hands of your own source of being and feel the strength of it, the power and elation of it, deflecting doubt in all its forms.

As you pass through hard times and good times, embrace your protection, open to your strength, listen for what you need to know. It is all there, all along the journey.

Understand that everything can be meaningful from the eternal perspective. You don't need to know how things will turn out or to associate your well-being with results. Hold on to the lifeline that connects you to the eternal. What can come through you is beyond your understanding but not beyond your knowing.

What you are here for is to allow the full experience of your eternal spirit to come through, undeterred by your limited perspective. Each condition and circumstance is a place of learning, if learning is what you desire. Much comes down to discovering what you want the most.

There is great adventure in finding your way. As you reach for it, you meet your beloved, you feel the grace you are showered with, and you begin to experience what it is to be fully alive and in sync with your eternal self.

As we grow in life, we develop a variety of tendencies, a personality unique to each one. Some of these tendencies may be self-destructive and others productive. The former block our way to our intended goals. The latter opens doors to creativity, insights and what we may have to offer others. So as individuals living with qualities that obstruct and those that flow, do we become stagnant? We have choices, but only when we recognize the source of the stagnancy and begin to understand the power of free choice.

The first step is to recognize the block to the freedom we seek. These blocks may be so familiar that they remain hidden from view. Recognition is the first step in making a good choice, to become free of the trigger reactions of fear, ambition, pride, self-doubt, the need for approval.

One must see the aberration to let go of it, often repetitively. Recognize it as the obstacle it is to what we want the most— the place of pure heart and the mind that embraces it—love and wisdom as one. So, first recognition, then choice, then courage, then the freedom to grow strong, to fulfill one's inborn potential, to fly. In a lifetime, there are obstacles and potential breakthroughs. Growing pains?

What steers one through the inner wars? The light of the longing for freedom, love, and evolution. Fear vs. Love: which one will win the case of our life? The jury is out; the judge is patient. What is unique is that the one on trial, so to speak, still has the choice, the chance to quell the warring factors again and again until the weapons are dropped and the war is dissolved.

In the battles of old, the General climbs the mountain to get a full perspective of the battle. In the battles within us, we are the General and the mountaintop is the place of peace within. Doubt and fear are generally related to something specific. Love and knowing are unrestricted. They allow us to live in open wonder.

Oh, what it is to be a human being! Obstacles vs. openings, all within a single human soul. All living beings eat for strength and eliminates for cleansing, but that same human being has some say about what to take in and what to let go of, and that makes all the difference.

Do not try to make sense of what you do not have the perspective to understand. You cannot fit the infinite into structures designed by the human mind. Let the experience of your heart be the guide.

Controversies are man made. They are the arguments of limited brains directed by multiple interests trying to bring the unlimited down to a size they can grasp and claim as their own.

When you see the trueness of spirit flowering, manifesting, lifting souls, appreciate it and marvel at it. Simply glory in that beauty's presence.

When you ask for help, lay no restrictions on how it must come. When you ask to serve, lay no restrictions on how you could be used. Different flavors add to the richness of the meal. Trust your response to the true.

"Always has been, is, and will be." Time meets timeless in a space where battles rage and are resolved all at once. Words of wisdom: stick with the timeless however you can and be part of its manifestation in the world of time.

Only you put the limits on that manifestation. Why? It's not your play. Leave aside what you cannot understand and enjoy what you feel with the knowing that surpasses the capacity of your brain.

Acknowledge and appreciate your good fortune and hold on to it even as you give thanks.

The doing that you have before you is actually about being, about the level of your consciousness. Focus on the being, and the doing that needs doing will flow from it naturally. The effort is to live as constantly as you can in a space where it can happen.

Not such a bad deal, you know! It's the very best there is. There is no rule that you have to be drawn off. Allowing yourself to be drawn off is, in fact, the only thing to fear. Let that one fear, based on your deep understanding, keep you in place or chase you back quickly if you lose your hold.

You get to practice this all day long. And, if it is your desire, you will learn. And as you learn, you can assist in the grand unfolding. You can be part of what is going on. There are no other obligations, because all that needs to happen will flow forth of its own accord from the highest place of your being if you are but connected to it. The actions you perform while you are in that place will be the results of what comes through you; and what those actions cause, in turn, will be for the good whether you are aware of it or not.

You can rest in the knowing that all is well.

You begin to observe obstacles dissolve as if by magic. Things you have wanted are gently falling into place. Yet all those things, as much as you appreciate them, are not the gift. They are more like the wrapping, the beautiful appearance, of a gift being given and received. The gift itself is the exchange of love with the infinite one, the feeling of the joining, of the energy moving through you to where it needs to go. That is all there is to want and as much as anyone can receive.

The gift enriches other incidences of human enjoyment, but only as long as you understand that they are incidental, and you remember always the object of your core desire and the source of your true delight. That one delight allows and even spawns many others.

No person and no event can take that gift away as long as you reach out for it, want it, appreciate it, let yourself go to it. You do not know how it will look—this gift manifesting—but you will always recognize how it feels.

New understandings are the offspring of new struggles. You have life—a gift to be prized above all else, for out of the cauldron of life rises the phoenix. As you go forward in valuing the gift, the choices become starker, even as they gain in subtlety. Each time you forget that what you have within you conquers all, you are lured into sadness, fear, doubt, and all their friends. Like a diamond untouched by raging flames, its sparkle and shine is there beneath the coating of soot.

A lot is going down in these times. Many early dreams are no longer valid. Your ignorance is as vast as your knowledge. You think you know what would be a "good" thing. You don't because you cannot see the whole. That is your condition. You can experience infinity, but you cannot encompass it. You don't even know what it is. You are much like a newborn child that suckles at its mother's breast, depends on her for life itself, but knows little of the mother herself.

Contrast is on the increase. Have and have not is being redefined. The only way through the turmoil is to curtail your mental meanderings into future possibilities and past perceptions. Listen in the stillness. Connect to the source of peace within you throughout your day and receive.

When you feel compassion, let it not be sympathy, but love. When you don't know what to do, doing nothing can be the wisest course.

When you feel overwhelmed, see it as a warning that you have forgotten your purpose, have taken upon yourself responsibilities that are freely offered from all around but are not yours. When you feel fear, remember your protection. When you are besieged by frustration or intolerance, know it as a sign that you have placed too much importance on outside affairs, how they appear, and how others appear.

All that you control is your choice to hold on to the hand that guides you through the maze. So utterly simple. So immensely challenging. Good thing you have help.

When you see that you have gone off track, take the time to see how that happened and set yourself aright. Then drop it, pure and simple. Let it be gone, or it will continue to drag you down. The presence never leaves you. That is what it is— present. You alone do the leaving.

Listen up. You are used to taking the routes of escape from all the "nasties" you encounter, even the little ones that aren't much to bother about in themselves except that they accumulate like dust.

Now it is you who are invited to be present within the presence by asking that it may flow through you. As you seek that way of being in your life, everything is always new, even when it feels familiar. Each surface the light falls upon reflects it differently, including you.

Your guide is the feeling, and when it seems distant or muddied, you have the tool of your effort. This is not about being good or bad. It is just about being.

Where, how, and with whom do you want to be?

Think about the word eternal. Like the presence, it has that "alwaysness" about it. The spark of the eternal resides within you. It is as strong and utterly powerful in one circumstance as it is in another. Learn to count on it and fear neither boredom nor danger, for they are conditions that pass. Seek all manner of help and know that it comes to you instantly, whether you recognize it or not. In receiving, you are giving; and in giving, you receive. It's a pretty spectacular arrangement, actually.

One focus can sit atop all others. Hold on to it. One love beats its drum through peace and chaos. The light of it points the way through any fog. Wait for clarity, and when you feel it, question not.

You have to start at the top, from the mountaintop, from the place where the presence reigns, then bring that with you into the apparent struggle of human beings.

Being. Start from the silence of being, just being. It is from there that you can begin to be who you are. It is from there that anything is possible. It takes practice.

The challenge is to let what IS be as it is without projecting your concepts onto it. Whatever you can see confines and constricts. It looks like there are many paths while there is only one. So much to let go of and so much to receive in its stead.

Sometimes you need reminders that put your journey into perspective. Your journey is one of redemption, of returning to your rightful state. Along this journey, there appear to be happenings—some that bring you delight, a sense of well-being, some that disturb in a variety of ways. There is, in fact, only one happening that occurs over an unimaginable expanse of time. It has no location, for it moves throughout all.

The light of the whole is the energy of being. It permeates every opening, calling itself back to itself. In the simplest of terms, that is your only concern—opening to that light, now and evermore. There is nothing that is not about that, be it birth or death or all that goes on in between.

The meaning of everything, anything, can only be seen in that context. That one understanding dissolves the complexity along the journey into the simplicity of one. Let your heart fill with the joy of that and be thankful.

As you live this life, you have the privilege of seeing the unlimited manifestation of this light of one in the many. Yet, this privilege or opportunity requires your acceptance and attention. That is your part in the grand unfolding of evolution. Which part do you want?

The more you see how the little choices, some that you fail to even notice, impinge upon your overarching choice, the clearer you will be about what furthers you along your way and what holds or pulls you back. Good and bad are not inherent in most actions. They are determined instead by motive and effect. There need be no down times. Each moment of life offers you equal opportunity to feel the touch of the beloved, whether it is in relaxation or fun, learning or accomplishment, even in pain.

As a matter of fact, the whole way most people determine importance and value is skewed by lack of understanding and, perhaps, the desire to be able to judge. You are not the judge either of yourself or others. You can assess, be drawn to or repelled by what you see, and most importantly, you can learn what serves your main purpose. The burden is off you, the opportunity before you. You grew up with the view of "should" and "shouldn't." The larger view is one of "would" and "could"—will and choice.

You are a lover and you are loved. You can be with your beloved always. That relationship is not limited by time or space. It is the oldest story in its highest form: attraction, engagement, coming together, creating—forever and ever. That is fulfillment. The eternal lover courts your attention, receives the tiny drops of your love, and brings them into the ocean of creation.

As you go through the seemingly petty aspects of your day, your simple awareness will open to you the very possibility for which you exist. Do you want to miss that? All you have to do is be there without conditions. What do you want? You know the answer to that. Be greedy for it.

Feel the tingling of all your physical cells as they are awakened and brought to life by this great merging and emerging love. With no anticipation, venture into what you have not experienced before and let it be what it is as it opens you further and takes you where it will.

So gentle are the hands of healing that massage the yearning soul, filling the openness with the beingness of the eternal. Understanding seeps in and radiates outward on beams of wisdom that far exceed the powers of explanation. The emanation of perfection radiates through imperfect beings who welcome it with love and trust, even as they stumble along their path of learning. The secret is to receive with openness without grasping, just allowing the filling to happen. Effort and enjoyment, yes; management, no.

You are evolving into what you are. And how would you understand what that means? Mostly by the feeling of it. The vision or the perspective that is unfolding before you is of an unfathomable vastness. Yet it is not an expanse of chaos, but rather of essential ordered unity.

That which IS encompasses all the diversity of existence. Your heart's desire is the magnet that draws you toward the one, and the energy from that one gives you the power to respond to the pull so that you are both drawn, or inspired, and left to choose how to move on step by step. That is the essence of evolving, expanding, becoming.

What may seem foreign is also innate. It is a process of discovering what you know from the place within where you have the opportunity of transformation.

Feel the love that holds you, acknowledge it, and be grateful. Then allow it to manifest through you, beyond you. Feel the strength that gathers within you, accept it, and be grateful. Then invite the giver of that to work through you. That is the expression of gratitude in action.

Through disciplined inner practice, you receive. Through listening, you see your way. Through words and actions, the flow of ongoing creation moves through you as you go forward on your path. That is the unending gift for you to open and be open to. It is what takes you out of the circle, as in going around in circles, and lifts you into the upward spiral of returning home. It is a journey not to be missed despite your eagerness to get there. That is why and that is the way you can greet your moments with equal delight. Each is the opportunity you seek.

There is almost always something to do, but we forget that at the same time there is always something to be. The quality of being that we bring to our doing is what makes all the difference. It has the power to transform the doing, to take it into the world of experiencing the flow of life in its profound beauty. It provides a place from which to observe as opposed to becoming tangled, to create instead of resist, and to feel joy as opposed to boredom.

Why prioritize the doing? Why let it be the ordering factor in your life while the very source of your life awaits inclusion?

You can be filled with the essence of your being as you carry out what needs doing. The reverse can be problematic. It takes trust to give precedence to the being part, to recognize its power to transform—a power you do not control, which can be a challenge in itself. But it is also part of the beauty, the joy of the unexpected that you alone could never bring about. As you give up trying to control what happens, to avoid what you see as bad, you begin to move into a new dimension. So-called problems give you practice. And as with most things, "practice makes perfect" or at least makes a step in that direction.

As you immerse yourself in "have to's," you resist and isolate yourself. You forget that you are loved, even so. This kind of love is not withdrawn when you make mistakes, what you know, or even turn away.

It can't, by its very nature. Your experience with others makes that hard to believe, but then you also don't notice your part in the separation.

You are loved as you are. Can you love others as they are? The heart that is recognized and relied upon does not need protection because it always has the love that has no limit. That love follows its nature and urges you to follow yours.

Appreciate the infinity of an instant. Instants naturally flow together, but as you appreciate them, they reveal themselves as passages to your own evolution. Give them precedence over all the "goings on" and the feelings they evoke, and you will begin to recognize your capacity for joy and the unimagined gifts it offers.

The joy of recognition knows its way through all the difficulties that a human life presents. Joy reduces them to gentle speed bumps. It just needs to be allowed to exist, to be free. It awaits your recognition, your attention, patiently.

Are you curious?

Sometimes when there are serious problems or perceptions of such, the characteristic human response is to get entwined with them, mentally and emotionally. The person with the "problem" is incapacitated by it, losing the distance that would provide any chance of finding solutions.

Stand back from the perceived threats that the problems present. You need a ground to stand on that lies outside the turmoil, where you can see clearly and seek your response with a calm mind.

Often problems even lead to new opportunities but not if they crowd the space where you can understand that while you are perplexed, you are not threatened from the long view. The place of safety is a place of consciousness within which you are removed from the threat, can find a longer-term perspective, and access your strengths.

You have that capacity. The first step is to take back your power—the power of the long-term view, the long-term purpose for your time on earth. Find your compassion, trust in your undisturbed insight, the grace that has shadowed you all your life.

Find your place in the situation, which is always unique. It is not one of confrontation, reaction, anger, or fear. It is one of clarity, love, and inner knowing. When all our carefully laid plans and expectations for our future begin to fall apart, there is no need to fall apart along with them.

We struggle to build security in the physical, but, as evidenced repeatably, the physical is fragile. Earthquakes, hurricanes, wars, depressions, accidents, and health issues all weave their way through essentially unpredictable lives.

So where is the strength to endure, now and in the future? It is in the spirit of the human being—the ability to find peace during conflict, to endure tragedy, to love and be loved, to find the place of balance even as the puzzle pieces fly off in different directions.

We build our futures in the present, but that future is illusionary and offers false security. We look for control but forget to turn to the only control we have. When global uncertainty rolls in, we can turn to the invisible solidity of our own inner strength in order to seek new pathways of commonality and unity. Who knows what could come of that?

The awareness of inner strengths, of the inner heart of peace, illuminates the power of choice. In the field of choice, the battle begins between the longing of the heart and the lure of apartness with its minions of fear, greed, and the false promise of control. The first seems risk-filled but offers stability, creativity, and joy. The second may seem stable but results in disintegration and destruction in the long run.

The ability to make choices leaves life direction in the hands of the individual. What will motivate the choices that chart the course of a life? Attention and awareness within the moments of the stream of life. Attention is fueled by will and consciousness. The stream of one life and its myriad of choices, often conflicting, is but a tiny part of the stream of ongoing life.

Along this journey, the choices do not demand loss of control of attention and motive. It just requires an understanding of what the individual cannot have effective control over, what happens in the cycles of existence around us.

You are unique among all who exist, as is each and every other. No one sees, feels, or understands as you have the capacity to do. You are here to be who *you* are, not who anyone else is. There is nothing of another to strive for or to compare yourself with. Aspire to be the one you are and to manifest that one in the consciousness that comes when your outstretched hand is touched by the caress of the unlimited.

All that you need is in a state of constantly flowing to you. It is for you to see these gifts and accept them. The human mindset is to view everything from a state of lack. Life is spent reaching, struggling, hoping for what is perceived as not yet being there. So, you live in a constant state of, "More, more, more."

See what you have, and you will want no more than to keep seeing, accepting, opening. It is for you to allow those gifts to open up, and you do that by living in the fullness. There is nothing to strain for and so much to appreciate. Do you know that truly? Is that place of knowing the place from which you view everything?

The consciousness from which you can see truly is not contaminated by the negative, by any feeling of not having, needing, sorrow, or fear. You say that you want it all, but do you know that you have it? Your work is to live in and from that acceptance.

Come out from under the rock and feel the sun shining down upon you, the rain of grace pouring over you, the immensity of the love filling you. Let that which is all come in and then emanate out from the unique one you are.

So do not ask for what you think you need but see that you have it and accept it. Let the song of your prayer be one of gratitude, for it is true gratitude that opens the door for receiving and knowing what you are receiving. Let that be your concern rather than all you see as problems, lacks, hurts, ailments.

As you go about living your life, walk in the consciousness of perfection, for no less than that awaits your acknowledgement. Perfection is something you let go to surrender to. And when you do, it shines forth from you as a pure note in the divine symphony.

Walk lightly in this world for you are tethered not to the ground you walk upon but to your spirit that is anchored in the realm of its source. You have been born upon this earth to be a star of love, a reflection of compassion, but you must accept it first.

Accept what is until you see the perfection in it, for each discordant element, by its very repulsiveness, points you in the right direction, and you begin to understand that there is no lack, even as you walk through a place where it seems to be everywhere. Lack, by definition, is absence. Yet in any moment, unconditionally, you can be in the experience of present, for that's what presence is.

It is a matter of focus, of attention, of observation. Lack and absence act like vacuums, drawing substance into them. In the life that you live here, you are subjected to that tug of war. But you can throw your own strength in either direction, and that is what makes the difference.

Sometimes you may feel so weak that you think you have no strength. That is when the core desire of your heart draws strength from its source, and you are protected and literally saved—drawn toward the one you seek to know, to be with, and to serve, even when you have forgotten.

So, walk lightly, with a light heart, and be thankful. Set your GPS for home and listen for the way, turn by turn. The GPS knows the shortest route, even as it changes with new conditions.

*Y*ou look at each day, each precious span of time that is offered to you, and you think about your agenda—all the things you need to do, feel you have to do or ought to do. Sometimes there are the things you *want* to do or things to busy yourself with to avoid thinking about what you *don't* want to do. All this doing! And it's all organized around your limited, self-centered view. These are hard words, but they are lifesaving words as well.

There is one "doing" designed to take precedence over all the others, and that is raising your consciousness. It has more to do with *being* than doing, at least initially. Reach up to the place where you can be filled with the wisdom, the light, the love—no less than the energy of creation. Melt into that energy. Be in that place of being, and your actions, however menial, will flow from there. Often, what those actions are doesn't really matter, just the place of consciousness from which they are taken.

Your purpose is not about what is going on in your life, although there is great purpose in your being where you are. You have felt the power of the energy radiating into you. It needs to come *through* you. It will heal you along the way, with each step you take to let go to it, but its purpose is so much more than that.

The power of that energy circulating through a human life is the same in any set of conditions—order and chaos, wealth, and poverty, all the opposites. Let go of your temporary purposes, and they will be taken care of more beautifully than you can imagine. Submit the energy of your life to the purpose beyond what you can see. It takes no more and no less than that.

The task is huge, all encompassing. If you try to handle it, you quickly find that you cannot. If you simply give your best effort, you will have a blast—and something will happen out of it, whether you see it or not.

Be open to receiving the gifts that you haven't known to ask for but can feel flowing into you. There is no need for you to know more than that a gift is being offered. All that is required is to be there in openness, to receive with unquestioning gratitude. You are given what you need even when, or especially when, you do not know what that is.

The gifts you cannot name or understand you can still receive as you float outside the restrictions of your human state to be encompassed by that which IS, always. This kind of gift, when it comes, is self-opening. Your role is to disappear into it, letting go in your consciousness the things that pass—all cares and burdens, fears, and restrictions—so that you can become a point from which light can shine out. The only doing for you is to hand over the deed to the temporary vehicle in which you move in time and let go to the unlimited that would shine through the tiny point that you are without the clouds of your interference.

You are literally carried into this space of being one and undivided, free of other associations and doings, and the light of that is what can be reflected to others as you interact with the people and situations of your current life. How would you see them from the consciousness of that unity? How would you engage with them if your sole purpose were to be a lamp lit with the eternal flame?

You have felt it. It is not unknown to you. Let your prayer be to learn how to see from that place of being, act in response to the flow that could pour through you. Learn how to disappear in it until you embody what you were created to be without imagining what that would be. The way is outstretched before you, and the life simply invites you to be in it, to reflect it.

It makes the array of happenings, feelings, and desires seem petty and inconsequential, doesn't it? They are there so you can learn, so that you can transform, and so that you can serve. Learn to carry your shelter with you and to run back quickly any time you stray. All is in hand. Enjoy the blessing of that.

If what you truly want is to serve your higher purpose— *the higher purpose*—you will need to learn to be open to it all day long and even while you sleep. It all becomes one thing. Go ahead with your day, responding to the needs that arise. Just bring to them your awareness; allow the flow to move through you into whatever business is at hand. You will begin to discover a whole other way of seeing, responding, giving out.

Awareness of what? Of all you are given to see from your highest place of being, but mostly of the power, the beauty, and the unfathomable love of the one you know but cannot name.

It's actually easiest to begin with a purposeful recognition when you first wake up in the morning. Feel the love and return it; feel the gratitude of your heart; put your day into the hands that guide you. Renew your will to serve.

Your purposes are fine. Just be open to the larger one so that they may be part of it. Know that the moments of your being are of equal importance, even though the whole structure of your view undermines that understanding. The structure that allows you to prioritize is okay too. Just know it for what it is, a tool.

Don't even look at problems until you can get into a place where there are none. From that perspective you understand that you are not bound by outcomes; you have no stake in results—nothing to hold onto except your own connection.

Learn to deflect judgments coming at you by not taking them into yourself. There is only one judge that matters. You can help steer the ship if you can become a wheel that the captain turns. Do not speak until you are clear. Stay in the flow of the power and energy that is coming to and through you and trust the outcome.

When you encounter a "difficult" situation that might strike fear or anger within you, or grab hold of you like a sickness, or even one that stimulates your desire for ego-centered gratification, you are actually encountering a pivotal learning experience. Recognize it as such, for if you choose the path of learning from it, you will have already begun to step back from it. You will have chosen learning over reacting, and there is great freedom in that.

There are questions to ask and to answer with the deepest honesty you are capable of. The act of asking the questions is another step away from the hold the situation has on you. Some of the questions might be:

- What do I have to learn from this?

- What do I have to give to others involved?

- Why has this attracted my obsessive attention?

Where does my attention need to go that I may be free, that I may move into the position of observation without contamination?

- What is my role, if any, in shifting negativity into resolution for myself and others involved?

Along the Way

As you come to answers to your questions, there are choices to make. It is a choice to let go of judgment even while you find the freedom to assess. Judgment is personal. Assessment is objective. It is a choice to put the *overall* good ahead of your own perceived good in the immediate. Each of the choices that show up for you has the power to free you or further enslave you. You will understand the nature of these choices by their results, and as you do, you will often find that you make adjustments accordingly.

No one said this was an easy road.

*R*emember as you live this life immersed in a present situation with all its connections to others, its particular history, and potential futures, that this life is one of many, many others. You may ask what or who is the one that has continued on through all those scenarios. Who is the actor, if you will, who is so immersed in each role that he forgets who he is outside of that role?

Who is that essential you but a precious soul learning the way step by step to maturity, fulfillment. Fulfillment of what? Fulfillment of the core longing that defies definition but that drives each one along the road back home.

Remember this when you feel like a captive of circumstances. The essential quality of circumstances is that they are all transient, just as the life you are living in time is transient.

What you seek is the eternal that shines through all the changes. And even more amazing is that you have what you seek. You can be with it, know it, accept, and return its love with yours. You are being taught how to be here in this life while connected to your eternal home at the same time.

It all takes patience as well as strength and determination. And it helps to remember the long view—one soul on one journey through many lives to one destination with instant help available for the asking. Each so-called difficulty is potentially invaluable—a chance to discover the keys to your success, to strengthen your protection, to reaffirm your choice. The secret is to ask for help before you are entangled. Be curious about what is to be learned, what is the hidden gift.

No element of evil or badness has power over you that you do not allow. That's why you need to see them clearly, recognize them for what they are. Then their allure can be dissolved in the light of truth, in the face of the gift that outshines all others. From that consciousness, you can have anything with impunity, because it is no longer yours or about you. Let it be.

There is a complex system within each human being that is essentially designed for your protection, your survival. It is seated within your ego-based persona. It has automatic responses for immediate protection—physical systems within your body. But it also has systems that are developed in response to your experiences in life, your perceptions of what is important to you, what you strive for, and what you protect against.

This automatic network has its purpose. Yet, as it is based in perceptions, it is restricted by the limitations of your view as an individual encountering particular circumstances within a minute chunk of all that exists in both physical and nonphysical form.

It is within this narrow environment that you make choices, and those choices can further define your path, can even narrow future choices. That said, understand that these systems are not bad. As you see more clearly the mechanisms of your personality, you may begin to understand how they developed. Stay as free of judgment of yourself as you strive to be of others. The clarity of that seeing enables new choices that you can then make consciously with deeper understanding. It allows you to replace reactivity with the freedom of conscious choice.

When you become aware of obstacles, be they inner or outer, you have the option of circumventing them. Many simply dissolve once they are noticed. Others take work, for they have deep roots.

Let's say you have a perceived need to be admired by others. That likely began very early in your childhood when it might have been a real need. You might now see that it isn't a real need for the path that you have consciously chosen. It may even have become an obstacle. Noticing, you can simply turn your attention toward what *are* your real needs. In doing so, you create a new habit that is rooted in your gift of free choice.

Turning away from the familiar toward the innate but less familiar can be wonderfully liberating. It takes an investment of trust and commitment, but the returns are astounding, even astronomical in the sense of being connected to that which is beyond your understanding. The mere effort activates swift support that you can feel and recognize even when you do not know exactly where it comes from.

A baby is tended by a loving mother long before it can mentally understand "mother." Hunger is satisfied, distress is soothed, needs are met by one whose perspective exceeds that of the child. But the child can receive, feel, accept, bond, and eventually trust. So can you.

It is a big learning, this one that everything is about one thing. In the foreshortened perspective of a human being, there are so many "abouts," so many desires, so many things deemed good or bad.

It is easy to get tangled in the maze of conflicting motives driven by the complex and often confused perceptions of what you want, what is desirable, what is important. Without this unifying perspective of "Everything is about one thing," the tangling continues, confusion grows, and satisfaction is temporary at best.

The very world you live in is in a state of breakdown. It is not your task to put it together again. Adjust your sights. Listen and follow your personal call. That is the only way through the chaos.

What do you seek? Truly. Know what you need, what you long for. What you want at the core of your being lies always within your reach and in great abundance, no matter what happens to be manifesting.

Pain comes as the body breaks down. What do you do with that? Resist? Engage? It is fine to seek solutions, but at the same time, take the opportunity to see beyond conditions. Learn what lies before you to learn as you walk single pointedly along your path. Ask to be shown the way and do your part to see it, understand it. The teacher is persistent, but the student is daydreaming, and the "problem" remains unsolved.

When you are focused single-pointedly in meditation, a feeling of fusion replaces *con*fusion. There is a coming together first of you with you and then of you with the eternal creative source of all. In that fusion your own self is not lost but rather expanded into another level of consciousness, of unity, of seeing.

For a time, you become what you are, for nothing intervenes. That which you are is a part of a whole that is infinite; it is beyond what you could hope to grasp, for that in itself would limit it. As you let that wash over and through you, you are enfolded into the whole and filled with its energy and light to the extent of your capacity in that moment.

That is the precious and indefinable possibility lodging within you and each one—even those who deny it. The challenge of your life, what it is all about really, is to explore that possibility and the opportunity it offers to engage in the endless cycle of giving and receiving.

Begin to see what your moments truly are in the infinite context. Understand that they are *not* about the outcomes, accomplishments, and desires of your life in the limited context in which you generally see them. They are about a potential way of being, now and forever. Hold on to that perspective, for it enhances learning, growth, and what you have to give.

Know what you know and how you know it, but trust what you cannot fully understand to unfold for you over time, as you become free of your own limiting ideas. You receive what you need to know, not what you cannot. Feel your way. It will show up for you step by step.

Sometimes you wake up feeling out of sorts, looking at your day and seeing nothing fun in it, nothing but drab routine. It is a correct assessment no matter what you see before you. The exhilaration of your life comes from what you draw down into it rather than from the people and events that are in it.

The magic, the sparkle you long for, is generated from your connection to that which is eternal. The power of that can light any space of darkness, enliven any day, lighten any burden, ease any pain, deepen any joy.

Your learning is well under way. Each day, no matter how dull it looks, can be filled with the gifts of discovery, for it is filled with possibilities you may not be seeing. Look for them with confidence that they are there. Soon you will see that the gifts are not in the props or the actors on the stage that invite you to believe in their play.

The grand prize is to behold the miracle before you with the eyes of inner knowing. The joy comes from how you live your life, not what goes on in it. Your very best opportunity to see that is actually in a time when you are not likely to attribute it to anything else. So even a day that looks empty to you is a gift in itself. Take advantage of it.

When you feel dry, your work is to drink deeply from the reviving waters of spirit. When you feel lonely, your work is to embrace the fellowship of those who share a similar purpose. When you feel stuck, your work is to ask to be anointed with the miraculous balm of eternal love.

Whatever you feel that is apart from that one you were created to be — lay it out in the sun. Recognize it first and let it go. See the dividers for the thieves they are.

There is a reason you walk through a world of negativity. And that reason unfolds itself before you in increments as you reach beyond that world, even as you walk through it. You feel the current, delight in the presence, wonder at the deliverance, the freedom, the joy as it passes through you.

This is a lifeline for you and others. It takes dedication to keep it intact. Be alert to any fraying of the rope, any blurring of the view, smudges on the window.

However, you choose to see it, your single purpose is to be a conduit, and that is far more about being than doing. All the help that could be awaits your request and your willingness to learn, to evolve. The process is one of receiving and enacting. Fill up with the gifts you can neither number nor name and carry them with you. As you use these riches, they regenerate.

When a gift is offered, accept it, and hold on to it. Allow the moments of your life to flow from your highest consciousness with the willingness to follow their lead and see what happens. You may end up ignoring something that seemed important, while others will be tended. Remember not just what you know, but what you don't know. You know something of your heart's desire, but little of where it will lead you in the physical world.

Along the Way

The flow of the eternal energy of spirit is constant and is relevant to the minutest details, the very moments of your life. You have to choose between carrying the burden, which is based on the desire for approval, credit, and control, and becoming part of the flow. For that, you must make the effort to hold on to that connection all day, stay receptive and responsive, and recharge as needed.

What matters is not so much what you do or don't do, but the place from which you do it. Sound familiar? Just a little reminder. There is so much to see and understand if you stay open and aware.

What appear to be the hardest things become easy when their time has come.

*Y*ou wake after sleep, and the possibility of a day of conscious moments lies before you. They are not needed more in one situation than in another. Your moments are equal in importance, each a part of the whole.

With humility, acknowledge your ignorance; with the will of your heart, accept the wisdom that would flow through you. You are learning a new way, or one that is new to you. It is, in fact, the oldest there is. Like a child, let yourself be taught. Like a musician, stay tuned to the conductor. Like one who does not know the way, ask for direction, and listen intently. It is okay not to know the *how*. You are not alone in your journey.

It is nothing less than total surrender that is being asked, for that is the door to receiving, to joining, to giving birth, to ecstasy. Each day, see the moments before you as being equally precious. Discover how to live in the flow of them. And remember, it is not in *your* scheme of things that the moments are equal but in the larger scheme. None of the moments—not the wakeful ones, the ones of fear and confusion, the uncomfortable ones, even the painful ones—need to be pushed away. With your focus on the one, they will evolve and you with them. In the grand design, the many flows out from the one and back again.

The eternal dwells within the temporal, shining through the chaos of opposites as a beacon for each one who would see it, showing the way back in the everlasting now. Just behold, be in its hold. Submit to your own creation. There is only one story repeating in infinite ways within the forms of creation.

As the light shines, darkness dissolves. The base within you that can be proud, wants to take credit, and yearns to be appreciated, has its life within darkness. That which serves, adores, longs to return home is child of the light—the very light that dissolves the darkness. You live, for now, where the two coexist so that you may learn to embody the one and let the other fade away.

*Y*ou may have a family, a job, relationships, and a web of responsibilities—some given, and some assumed—but you have only one purpose. Focus on that purpose and listen for the signals, and everything else will fall into place naturally. Some things will fall apart, and some will come together. Some you may be immediately happy about and some may elicit concern or fear. Even the latter can be an essential part of the larger story of what you are here for.

Discover how your primary purpose can be fulfilled. The significance of each thing that happens lies in how you respond to it—whether from the context and perspective of forever or the context and perspective of the immediate.

Search for the view of forever and learn. It takes a deft shifting of gears. It takes remembering. And it takes the strength of your commitment. What it provides for you is solid ground to walk upon across stormy seas or boggy slush or through the densest fog. That is something you can count on.

A pointer: be selective about what and whom you engage with. No need to respond to every "email" that comes into your inbox. Some contain cleverly hidden viruses. Some show up because they are a part of your essential work. Discrimination is imperative, and there is only one way to come by it. It must be given. So "knock upon the door" and ask for help with a humble and earnest heart. Seek your one purpose and fulfill it in the moments of your life.

The more you can be clear about what you know and what you don't know, the more open you can be to each moment that presents itself. What you know most deeply you cannot name, for it *is* the name, or emanates from it. What you don't know are the possibilities before you that might not be, or usually are not, in accordance with your own projections and plans. You think you know what you are going to do next, and as long as you are glued to that, you will bully your way through to it, congratulating yourself for deflecting other options, staying focused.

The question is, what do you want to be focused on? What you know or what you think you know? There is a line of communication from a much larger perspective than you could possibly have, just waiting for you to be in listening mode. Your instincts are good, but you are so used to blocking out the unwanted that you often fail to recognize their promptings, to listen to the source of your wisdom.

You know the difference between a distraction and a prompt. Be the wheel of your boat, not the hands that steer it. Do you see the difference? You are a wheel with consciousness and choice, so you choose your captain. The choice is ongoing, made throughout the stream of your days. Is it informed by the default path of your own small view, or are you listening for the unexpected note in the maestro's symphony? Are you open? Ready? That alert listening and ready response is what gives wholeness to your life.

Along the Way

Do you have any inkling of how well you are defended, cared for, loved, embraced? That is given. It is for you to accept it, to be open, to stay tuned to the channel of the one you seek to serve.

Learn to leave room in your consciousness for the whisper of the original lover in motion, the fun of unrestricted letting go, where you can see and feel and hear the beloved within you and respond in everyday moments. There's nothing like it. Best-ever solvent for perceived burdens. Magical.

As you look around you from your life circumstances to those of your family, friends, and acquaintances and then beyond to the world at large, you can imagine no solutions to the complications, dangers, and downward spirals of tangled interconnections and divisions. And you are right. There are no solutions that your mind is capable of grasping, much less putting into motion.

That's why your work is ultimately simple in the sense of uncomplicated. Your work and your contribution are to hold on fiercely to the presence. That is the only source of resolution for what has evolved on this earth.

As darkness thickens, you can transmit light. Trust in the power of that with all your being throughout your waking hours and then hand over that intention when you sleep. Let that be your resolve and learn how to stick with it. There lies the ongoing choice.

Immerse yourself in the privilege and the preciousness of the gift of that simple work. Nothing else matters. Nothing. A little boy is said to have put his finger in the hole of a dyke and save countless lives. As the story goes, he just did what was there for him to do, through the cold and exhaustion without considering the impossibility of the outcome.

There is such joy at the core of steadfastness. So much unpleasantness slips off the smooth surface of the single-pointed mind and heart that refuses to engage the negative. Remember that your strength is to focus and invite the power that can move through you when you allow it. That power is infinite, whether or not you can see it.

You will find that as you practice attention and trust, you will know when there is something for you to do or say. It can become almost a reflex in the clear space of openness and awareness. You will, of course, have to sacrifice all that angst and those burdens, the fear and hopelessness. That's just the way it is. Oil and water do not mix.

Effort is rewarded, knowing is quickened, and connection is strengthened as you make your way as best you can. Everything matters, each moment. A smile offered from heart-space can be of far more importance from the larger perspective than something else deemed to be a major accomplishment in the restricted view of you and others.

You can make something good out of anything and everything, even if it seems very small. It may take all of your strength, but never more than you find within you.

Let yourself be cared for. Let go of the stubborn urge to do everything yourself and enjoy the partnership offered by the infinite to the very rascal that you are. Just glory in it, even through the swirling ashes of destruction that may gather around your feet. Stand tall and watch the phoenix rise.

Let's say you have a day when you are not working on your job. Take the opportunity to focus on your own essential work, not on your "to do" list but on the quality of being that you want to maintain. Consciousness. Observe with gratitude but not judgment when you feel the presence that needs no name to identify it. See where you are pulled into what isn't, to lack, burden, annoyance—any form of negativity—and simply allow your heart to pull you back.

It doesn't matter what gets done. Let go of that part. Just spend a whole day with a single intention and watch. Once you observe the departure from that intention, the return to it is automatic if you catch it soon enough.

This is self-learning, like an online course. A nice metaphor implying that you have to stay online to be on course! That's the fun part of words.

The reward is the feeling itself, as well as the learning. When you recognize and accept your primary objective, all other worthy ones will thrive beneath it. There is nothing more efficient than the energy of spirit given full permission to manifest. But it helps to understand that you cannot anticipate how it will play out, where it will lead you in the immediate. Give it a chance. All day.

As you notice the flow that is your spirit joined with your very source, be grateful and give thanks.

From the space of no words comes the wisdom beyond words. It shines down upon the disparity of human souls, offering itself freely to all who would respond. When you are rooted in that state of knowing from which your own persona, with all its cares and doings, has withdrawn, then the words that come through to you carry the light of wisdom.

Rise above the worlds upon worlds of struggle and problems. Seek your knowing in the space where the victory has already been won, where there is no illness of body, mind, or soul. Be there and absorb the glory of it, where the brilliance of joy allows no shadow of doubt, and wait patiently.

Allow yourself to be filled with surety; claim it, and stay with it. Do your seeing from within the experience of the power of spirit flowing through you. Become a relay station.

A tool doesn't worry about outcomes. It fits into the hand of a carpenter so that he may build his house. The tool knows nothing of the house that is evolving but is essential to its building. In this mode, you can feel the happening, participate by choice, receive while you are making effort to give.

Like any house, you are in need of constant cleaning. And, yes, you are both a tool and part of the house—a unique position, which you are only beginning to understand.

Surety is both your security and that from which your security comes.

It all comes down to what purpose you wish to serve at any one time. You may have made an overall choice about what you want to do in your life, but the work of living here on earth is to bring that choice into the minutia of your days.

How easily you slip from the perspective of your best intentions into serving your immediate desires as they present themselves in all their endless forms. How you navigate through your days is fundamentally a matter of consciousness. You have so many automatic responses grooved in by habits formed in unconsciousness.

The first step is to slow down your momentum. Shift from autopilot, reactive mode, to the place of your highest intent and receive the perspective you need. Ask for help. Whatever you need is there, waiting for you to ask. You know that from repeated experience.

This is not wishful thinking. It is a matter of giving substance to your overarching choice, letting it guide and determine your actions, thoughts, words. The battle is won in little victories that magically become huge.

The discipline of finding your own quiet space, separate from the activity of your days, is key to being able to actually serve the purpose that you embrace in moments of inspiration and clarity but so quickly forget in moments of stress or obliviousness.

The help you need awaits your call.

The words or understandings that stream into you from that which you seek to serve are carriers of expanding wisdom. They are not static, but alive for those who are open to them. Different people will hear them differently as they open to new understandings and are faced with new situations. There is no right or wrong about them. You can relax about that. Yet, to listen for such understanding takes a certain letting go of your limited view so that it can be heightened to new levels.

The commitment of a life of service Is made continuously, not just once. Failing that, you pull away by degrees, lose the certainty out of which such a commitment must be made, and will need to begin again. You are learning how to walk, and, as for a child, much learning is needed. Each effort teaches you until the art of it becomes part of you.

Over the years of a lifetime, trust is pushed to the limit, but never beyond. Recognize that. Refine your understanding of what matters to you within the context of the primary goal of your life. As the external elements of security appear less dependable, you will either scramble to shore them up or turn to the only security that is inherently dependable.

From that place of acceptance, you create within you the freedom of independence, the wisdom to make choices, and the energy to power through all situations and conditions toward your true goal. Changes will take place, and they will either serve you or challenge you. If you take advantage of the challenges, they will end up serving you as well.

Know that you are in the best of hands. Know that you are guided. Know that you can be used as much as you allow. Know, too, that you don't always know the specifics of what is in your best interest. You can be grateful for far more than you realize. As a matter of fact, from one perspective, you can be grateful for everything. All circumstances and conditions can potentially play a part in your own transformation.

*H*ow do you find your own answers? How does a thought become not just a belief but a knowing? It takes openness first, and that openness comes from your own state of readiness—the place where your own sincere search has taken you. When you can walk through the door of openness, you enter the space where you can experience.

Your own experience is what leads you to knowing belief, if not total understanding. You know as you go. You feel the alignment or not. And when you do not feel it, take the time to see what is askew. That way, each step has integrity and solidity. The doubts that need resolution will show up for you, and if you examine them openly, can lead to deeper understanding. Those are more like questions than doubts, pointers to what needs clarification. The doubts seated in resistance will bounce off and do not need your attention. The forks in the road continue. The road signs are lit by your heart connection. Protect it with all that you have.

As you review your journey so far, parts of it may be repugnant, but each part can help your learning. It may take years to learn to distinguish between the trueness of the transforming touch of a loving god and the sometimes well-meaning attempts of others who may also have become aware of that touch but seek to manage and manipulate it. It is your sincerity that fosters your learning and leads you through that wilderness. And it always will. Let go of the missteps. They are being dissolved. The rest can stay.

You have chosen a life of learning. Trust the teacher when you recognize the teacher's voice, but, as is suggested, test your learning. Blind acceptance leads to sink holes, quicksand. Experience is the provider of your solid ground.

You may feel weak, small, even afraid, but that which comes to you is not. Let go of what diminishes and hold on to what expands.

Persistence. Without judging your success, keep turning to the unwavering true. The war goes on within and without, and it's not a pretty sight. Sometimes it is your very heart that is bruised by what you see. It is a danger, a backhanded way of pulling you into despair. Do not go there, either in disgust or sympathy, anger, or fear. Hold the sword of light. That's all. Walk in the world but be not of it. Be powered from your connection to infinite being, securing that source within your very core. It is the only way forward, the only way out of a tunnel of darkness.

Love is showered upon you. Let it soak into the places that hurt, that quiver, that get caught in confusion.

Trust that the pockets of darkness, the caves of negativity, will be cleaned out as you offer them up to the power of light. The tentacles of darkness reach out for the aspiring soul. It is good that you feel them and that they frighten you as that fear propels you in the other direction.

There are no problems save the ones you see as such, the ones you entertain even as the guest of guests comes to your door. Problems are fed with the attention you give them. As you extend to them belief in their power, you help to create their power over you.

Keep turning to the constant outpouring of love that comes to you with direction and purpose. Come to be healed, to be filled, to be evolved. Welcome the gift. It knows what to do, where to go. Rejoice.

The methods you have developed over time to live in what may have always seemed an alien world are no longer applicable. They were tools of preservation, essentially defensive in nature. As your understanding of why you are here grows, you need no longer live on the defensive.

The time has come to stand with confidence in the authority of the purpose you have basically accepted yet still resist. This is not about you; it is about what can come through you as you let it. You are allowed, yet you must allow.

The stream that would flow to and through you is constant. You need not always be aware of it, but you do have to leave the gate open. Be conscious of the eternal stream in the very moments of it. That is when it becomes truly yours once again, for you are no longer buffeted by events, other people, or undermining motives.

Lay down your sword. The wounds of past battles no longer need tending. Pick up the sword of light and trust it, not only in the high moments of felt connection, but always. No less is the goal. It comes down to your will and your choice, always. You alone can ask for the gift of giving. You alone can let go of your agendas that are so constantly in the making.

Conscious effort clears the way, the path to the truth and the light. It is time to expand your awareness, to perceive a new center of the circle, to let everything revolve around the one desire you came with. That is your new center of gravity. It is a shift as great as that of Earth shifting on its axis, but it evolves from the magnetism and power and singularity of purpose.

A time of seeing both the beauty and the ugliness is ahead. Keep on your path through all the pulls that would lead you astray. Allow and thrive. What goes through you also enriches you. It is a rather amazing arrangement. Very economical.

The great shift is from the ego of the little creature that you are that sees its world about as accurately as a cat does but with more confusion, to the ego of the eternal you, fashioned in moments outside of time as you know it. Hence your life here shifts from being about you to being about that. The choice is ongoing. The goal is for that choice to become a steady stream.

As a human being walking amidst the very battle between good and evil, giving and greed, serving the greater good and serving perceived self-interest, you have the power of choice. Intelligence of a kind unmeasured by man flows toward you upon your sincere request and your desire to use it in service.

The famed leap of faith is from the limited wiring of the human brain, along with the primitive conditioning of individual experiences, to the experience and acceptance of the mysteries of infinity. You fight that like a child driven by immediate wants and fears, but unlike many a child, you are not forced to succumb to superior wisdom.

You must choose. Once you have, of course, you are frequently protected from danger that you may not even be aware of. But in the day-to-day of your life, request help, acknowledge your need and your innate desire for connection and synchronization with your source.

The hand of the reaching soul is grasped instantly. The way forward is cleared, but it is you who must do the walking. So how does that play out in your life? The key is consciousness of your position and the opportunity of each moment that you are given. You can accept or reject. As you accept, you begin to open to that which you can know but not grasp.

The spirited but recalcitrant child that you are is often stuck in two-year-old mode—feeling the need to rebel in order to claim your developing independence. That is a habit from the past; you are beyond that now. Your independence is well developed, and you are left with the power of choice.

Build the house of bricks, young piglet, for the wind of the wolf is persistent and strong. Then dwell in that house. Bring it with you like a turtle as you move through the circumstances, conditions, relationships, and struggles that so often blur what you know to be the one path to move safely through them.

Talk about independence! In that seeming surrender, that core acknowledgment of your source, you find your unbounded freedom. You find your very own well of joy, your ultimate safety, the fulfillment of the one nonphysical desire you were born with. Think about what matters to you most and claim your gift of gifts.

Sometimes it is in moments of overwhelming fear and aloneness that a human being reaches out to their god in total desperation. And when that reaching happens from the depths of sincerity, the response is immediate. The person is filled with such an experience of well-being, beauty, glory, safety, love—that its imprint is life changing. It can be pushed aside but never fully forgotten because it is so utterly real.

What you don't realize is that that gift, that love, that unnamable and immaculate care, is waiting for you patiently—always. As you recognize the one thing you need and ask for help, it is granted in the moment of request if it comes from an earnest and sincere heart.

The gift of that is there for you now, enveloping you. Your acceptance opens up your space to receive. So, there are two doors—the one you knock upon that it may open to you and the one within your being that you must open first to be able to receive. It is as the coming together of true lovers—one that once came from the other and seeks reunion and the other who welcomes with open arms.

The joy of reunion, when it happens even in moments, resonates with a life of its own far beyond what you know. In receiving, you are giving; in giving you receive. That is the way of oneness.

Some people just need love of the purest kind with no demands, and you can give that in so many different ways because you have felt it yourself, received it yourself. Make that your focus rather than fixing apparent problems. All your doing can be in the rhythm of that tune of love. Ask to see how that can be. Just let it radiate through you. Get out of the way.

As you do that, the bits that are in the way will show up for you in the light so you can recognize them for what they are and let them go. The way is straight, and narrow is a blessing. A steady focus is your ride to the unlimited.

The something that everything is about isn't limited. What is limited is your openness to it, your utter trust. Like a child wanting to swim in deep water, the time comes when you must take the leap without a life preserver. Trust. What is your life preserver? And what could you hold onto instead? Something to think about.

How willing you are to accept the burdens that literally assault you as you go through your day, whether they come from your work, your home life, or your circle of family, friends, and acquaintances! Understand that no burden is yours to carry. Others send them to you to unload themselves. They are not yours.

You need to readjust your sight, your understanding of what you are here for, and do it often. So many have an agenda for you—those who love you, those who pay you, those who work with you, and even some of those who merely encounter you.

Yet it is the original agenda you were born with that you are here to fulfill. Once you put that first, it orders everything else. Do your primary work, and all else will be taken care of. The unlimited stands ready to flow through you, waiting only for your invitation. It can pour into any kind of work, any effort you make for another. You can do what seems to be unrelated entirely, and that which comes from infinite can still flow through you if that is your primary intent.

The work that you came here to do can manifest itself through all your actions, thoughts, even your very presence, as you engage with what you see to do or merely rest. It is up to you to put that work first, to allow it, to accept what you know that exceeds the range of your brain's understanding, even as you become more certain of it.

So, as you approach tasks or challenges, remember your ultimate goal. Do what you see to do from that perspective and let everything else remain untouched or incomplete. Just let them be. That one choice, that one work, is what brings unity to your life.

What is it that makes something matter? There is a lot to understand here if you want to. What makes something matter is that it has import in the grand evolution of creation back into the domain of its source. Creation continues to be in the process of being re-created.

Understand that you cannot understand in your human brain how this evolution is happening, and hence you have no basis in your brain to even guess what is for the better or for the worse.

What you can do is to give your attention to that larger purpose and consciously let it take its course. How? Never by thinking that you know what needs to happen, as so many do. It is from the place of letting go of those limiting concepts that you can feel, see, and know the right actions for you. Your effort must be to hold on to the highest state of consciousness you can. That's about it.

As you go about your day, let that be your single priority. When it is, you will not be thrown off course by happenings or the people around you that are not as you think they should be. Maybe they are and maybe they aren't as they should be, but it is only from the consciousness of your very own source that you can begin to fathom the larger picture and your role in it—to be a conduit for that spirit of being, that very light through which what has been created can evolve.

So, while it is clear that you don't know, if you let go of what you think you know, you can truly know what you need to know. Knowing in this sense is a state of being. It takes purity of heart, clarity of motive, and the unleashed power of the love that dwells within you.

Lay down the burdens and walk with a light step. Embrace your truth and let the light of it show you the way, step by step. You will be shown; you will be led; you will learn. One purpose, many ways of carrying it out.

So accustomed are you to being the center of your own universe with your perception of all creation swirling around you that it is a far reach indeed to see the radiant reality of the infinite. You are not expected to, but pray try to catch a glimpse of the magnificence of which you are an infinitesimal part and rest in the security of the timeless structure of creation. As small as you are, you have choice. Do you see how big that is?

Choice can lead you to an expansion of consciousness and the potential of eventual unification with or return to THAT from which all came or the opposite and all states between. The key choice is one of direction. Where do you want to head? What is the guiding desire of your being?

You have answered that question for yourself already. Where you trip up is by falling into that insane human habit of trying to sort out the mysteries of life through a system of rights and wrongs, goods and bads. There's no need for that. Remember the saying, "Love god and do as you please"? Focus on the love, the ultimate goal, and let everything unfold from that. Accept your infinitesimally small and infinitely essential part in the magnificent whole.

Sometimes you have to be stopped in your momentum so you can see how well life carries on without your efforts. You spend so much time trying to control your environment, your situation, the misperceived elements of your security. It is a futile endeavor, for these things cannot be controlled. You can and must interface with them, but as a free agent, a servant of your own destiny. And, no, there is no contradiction here. Hand over the controls to your essential spirit that shines with the energy of one and experience true freedom.

The waltz of love moves to the rhythm of the ongoing union, the ongoing creation. Listen for the music and let your heart go. Such a lovely heart. It already knows the way. Stop trying to bring infinity down to size and simply enjoy it as it is.

Are you enjoying the imponderables? Here is another one. Your higher self is where freedom (choice) and surrender (opening) become one. Talk about ecstasy!

A surrounding sense of unease comes as you are faced with the reality that you have little control over other people or most events. When you don't like what you see, the reality of that shatters the illusion you and most others have lived in—a sense of well-being based on "insubstantial stuff."

Put that up against the value of a life based on a reality you can depend on. You are not asked to trust on faith because of a supposed should, or even because there doesn't seem to be any alternative. Trust comes from experience. There is a trade involved. You let go of how things look, and the door opens for you to see how things are. Feel the solidity of that. Be grateful even for what may seem bad, for it pushes you toward your destiny.

And destiny, by the way, is not something foisted upon you. It is the result of the energy of your spirit moving along the way of its choice, directly or indirectly forging ahead. Honor that. Allow yourself a good long soak in the tub of gratitude, in appreciation for the substantial stuff that is lodged in your heart. It, too, can be seen. It has more solidity than any table or chair.

The stream of gifts flowing into you cannot be deserved. Just see them. Acknowledge them. Receive them fully, not just peripherally. They are everywhere. Gather them. They are magical. As you pass them on, they multiply within you. Keep your eyes on the "goodies," and the "baddies" will lose their bite. Cough up the negative ones that are lodged in the past so you can approach your now freshly.

Intense desire can bring forth powerful learning. It can feel disturbing, even confusing—new and familiar all at once. When you feel the coming together of your rising spirit and the gift that is showered upon it, you can just let go to it. It is a guided process, a kind of birthing that takes precedence over everything else.

Your part, as always, is choice and will, ongoing. You choose your direction out of your deepest longing and aspirations and power it forward with the energy of your will, enveloped in a plea.

Accept what you are given with gratitude, whatever the wrapping, as it is always crafted specifically for you. You cannot anticipate the response to your call, what it will bring forth, but you can trust it and discover the response it elicits from you.

When you ask to serve, it implies a willingness to follow direction, and to do that, you must learn to hear it. It's not always in in words! The presence is unmistakable to the open heart, and that heart just wants to absorb it, be with it. That is a state of being in which you can only be. It fills, purifies, expands, exhilarates, even possesses what you bring to it, and it has the potential of manifesting through you.

When it comes time for action or movement, you can carry the experience of that space of being with you. That is part of your current learning. It can become your normal, although as long as it is real, it will always feel new. Its nature is to evolve with you. Creation is still going on. How beautiful is that!

Part Two

Inner Dialogues

The journey before you is one of "realizing the presence." When you come to a place of simple acceptance of the simple truth, no harm can come. The outcome is perfection, even if it flies in the face of all the specifics you hope for in the small patch of reality in which you walk. The power and the glory live within you.

You cannot protect another, but if you wholeheartedly accept your own protection, you allow it to shine out through you. You have one basic purpose in your life. All others flow from that one. What is "good" is whatever takes you to unity, oneness, wholeness of being. What is "bad" is anything that you allow to pull you away.

I catch glimpses of the meaning of this, but sometimes it just seems too big. What I am trained to see becomes my focus instead of what I know to be. Fear, dismay, tangles of involvement with lesser goals are such powerful distractions.

Yes, they are. And yet it is those very elements that offer you the contrast that enables you to see, to feel your way. By their nature, they don't feel good. The quicker you identify them, the sooner your work can begin. You hold all the cards. The presence is never not present, even when you have turned your back. Ask for help. Make your effort as best you can. That is the stuff of becoming. The sooner you know that you have veered off the course, the shorter the trip back.

I need so much help with this! And I also acknowledge, here in this moment, how huge is the help I am given. I feel my heart filling with gratitude and awe, love, and yearning.

Offer up your doubts to the melting heat of the love. Each doubt that disappears makes more space in your cup. See that you allow that space to be filled with more love and not another doubt.

Please show me as I go along.

What do you think this is all about?

It is what I asked for, isn't it?

Yes.

Thank you. I feel sometimes that I don't know the first step.

The first step takes place from wherever you are. And you always know that much. Just begin, and begin, and begin again. Hold out your hand, and the steps will show up for you.

Hold out my hand.... I can do that. I will do that—again, and again, and again.

Not just steps, but micro-steps. Observe the little things that pull at you. See them for what they are before the pulling works before accumulation gets out of hand. When that happens, a little annoyance can flare into a forest fire of destructive anger.

What can be a sword of light becomes twisted and unwieldy, hurting both you and whoever else is around. The sword of anger, when it is called upon, is meant to serve as a surgeon's tool of healing. It must be clean to avoid infection. It must be used precisely by an experienced hand, with clear intent.

Emotions that accumulate gather force underground, undermining your best intentions. You have physical experience with accumulation; you know how it happens and how it feels. And you know as well the freedom of sweeping it away. Emotional accumulation is no different.

This can be so hard. When the hidden comes to the surface, it feels like poison. Confusion reigns, and clarity seems a distant call.

Trust and keep steady in your course. You cannot measure the distance you travel or where you are on the journey. Just take care of your moments, and all else will unfold seamlessly.

I am disturbed because I can't see the way.

You will when you need to.

Fear is a sticky soup of fog that rolls in uninvited.

It is made of insubstantial stuff —

> A fog of illusion,

> A black magician's trick.

I want to be free of it.

Why?

Hmm. I have to look into the depths for the truth of that. Part is wanting to be free of the discomfort of fear and to feel safe, even in illusion.

Yes.

Part is that I want to be what I was born to be.

A being with choice.

I want the freedom to follow my deepest longing, to live in the heart of the love that I have felt, to respond to the call that I hear.

It is a choice made moment by moment, in the face of whatever seems to be in the changing world. The choice is always the same and is often easier to make in times that show up as "hard."

What will help?

Instead of responding to the threat, step back from it and look for the gift. And when it seems hard to find, you could always ask for help.

Yes.

Remember the child's game of hiding something? When the seeker looks around, the one who knows where the hidden thing is says "warmer" or "cooler"? Those hints are there for you as you play the game of discovery as well. Listen for them.

I just need to listen?

Ask and listen, yes. And respond. Know that what you seek is there, waiting for you to show up.

It sounds so simple.

In reality, it is:

It takes being open to receive.

It takes trust to be open.

It takes longing to come to trust.

So, start with the longing.

Hold on to that. It is a horse that heads unerringly for home.

Thank you.

Any time.

Really?

Really! There is plenty to doubt—mostly how things look instead of how they are. Doubt all the things that lure you away from the one thing that has never failed you. We are back to acceptance.

Okay. Acceptance.

You are not in a position to judge the happenings around you, and yet how easily you fall into the old habit of allowing yourself to be lifted or dashed upon the rocks by them. Being drawn into negative thought and letting its toxicity affect your experience of life is one danger you can name as such with certainty.

As a new happening comes into your awareness—whether it is an event, a piece of "information," or another person's state—see it as an opportunity to fuse yourself to the knowing within you. Stand in your light with all the tenacity you can muster. Your effort rings the bell that calls for help, and help comes. Always. Has it ever not?

No one is suggesting that there are not bad things out there. The forces of disintegration and integration are related in the material world. Some things fall away before others can grow. The ultimate simplicity for the child that you are is to hold on to the parent with all that you have. You can relax in that space, play even, but not forget.

Oh my god!

You got that right! Just fasten your seat belt and hold on. You have more support than you are likely to ever know. From that place of trust, let your actions flow. Not reactions, but actions taken in the clarity of your deepest knowing.

It is all about ONE. One thing to do, one place to be, one thing to hold on to, one thing to let come through you—one thing to experience in all its forms. It is simple beyond reason, or you might say, beyond reason is where you see the simplicity. Lighten up, literally. From within the light, the way is easy. The mountain can move; the water can part or be stepped upon.

You have an invitation to come to the party, and an RSVP is requested. Transportation will be provided. Come as you are.

So, it's a school, a challenge, a roller coaster ride, a situation where only one thing matters, and a party!

Yup, among other things.

"Good grief!" said Charlie Brown.

Well, he was wrong about that. Joy is the better option. Fun is pretty good too. It is what happens when you know that the rest is in good hands. And what better?

There is a reason you walk here on earth. You haven't the means to understand it fully, but you do get your feet dirty in the process. All that is other than that which you seek abounds, surrounds, calls to you. As you become clear about what pulls you away with false promises, you are positioned to choose and to know what you are choosing.

You have watched babies learn how to walk. Such effort, such single-mindedness, through tears and laughter. The child is propelled by an inner instinct that is built in. You have it too—the instinct, or rather the need, to move toward the "arms" that await you. You will stumble and you will get up. Your heart knows the true as a compass knows north. Let it show you the distinctions between what you thought you needed and what you do, between fool's gold and the real.

Please show me the difference as I go. It seems that past hurts and fears hover around me, looking for the cracks in the armor of my will.

Remember that what will be IS in the world of one. As you are in forward movement, feel and absorb and reflect what IS. Be propelled by that, by the fullness rather than the lack. See what you have; be what you are; embrace what is offered; appreciate the love that pours into and through you. It is when you see what already is and always has been that it expands within you and moves through you. As the sports coach says, "Keep your eye on the ball."

Judgement is fine when it means having "good judgement" or common sense. However, it is lethal when it is a matter of judging yourself or others. In that mode, "good sense" generally disappears. The judgement goes beyond the capacity of the judge, but this is so common that people hardly notice it.

What they do is build fences around people, including most particularly themselves.

The "sentence" has been passed, and one lives with it, never fulfilling one's potential. Sometimes, we are afraid of our own potential, largely because we haven't experienced it yet, at least in a steady way. We get glimpses of what could be, but since it hasn't developed, it is unfamiliar and, as such, even frightening. We are used to how we think we are, making that definition self-fulfilling. It may be less than it could be, but it is familiar.

As soon as a baby bird is ready to fly, its mother pushes it out of the nest where it must fly or die. The vast majority fly as they were born to do. What were you born to do? To be? How will you ever know if you hold on to the fear of flying, of going beyond yourself as you have defined that self?

It takes great courage to break through the containers that you and others have placed around you and defined you with. What would happen if you threw them out? You don't yet know that undefined self, what it is like, what it could offer. We learn to be "humble," to accept our limitations. It's not that everyone doesn't have them, but that we tend to engrave them in stone, limiting the potential to advance beyond them.

Breaking through these "containers" is the essence of freedom. But you embrace the familiarity and seeming safety of limitation. You are invited to leave the nest of your own volition. To the extent that you accept that you don't know what that will be like, you shed your limitations and open the door to your own unique evolution.

Absorb the love everlasting that is yours to receive. Melt into it, and let it do what it does as it passes through you to others. Just don't allow yourself to imagine what that might be like. There is no model to imitate. You simply discover it in the silence of no words. It's like a surrender to your eternal self.

I have no idea how to do that!

That's a start! You only need to be open.

I've always had standards to judge by, even without knowing it.

Yes, and they continue to hold you back even as you instinctively resist them. In fact, what are your obligations? Think about that. There seem to be so many, but which comes first? Which one allows the others to fall in place with clarity? Which is your priority that comes before the others, even allows you to fulfill the others?

As an adult tasked with seeking your own sustenance, turn to awareness without judgement. It is rich, nourishing, and non-restrictive. In fact, it is freeing.

There is a hurt so deep that I cannot cover it. I can neither push it away nor ignore it. It wants to eat me until I am no longer.

Yes, there is a wound that has been carried through many lifetimes.

I need to put it down, yet that frightens me. How would I be without this defining scar? I don't know how it came about, but I cannot remember life without it.

It began many lifetimes ago and found renewal in each succeeding one, differently each time.

How can I be free?

Let go of it. You are ready for it to heal because you are strong enough now. Let the fight come out, the power of your will. As we said before, "Come out from under the rock." You are ready. You have the tools and strength to walk on this earth with your eyes open, without a crutch, and with a singularity of purpose. You have only one essential need, which is repeatedly met for the asking. The others are for you to take care of. The power of your will is on the rise. Use it.

Another choice lies before you. Trust your clarity instead of throwing a blanket over it. The truth can be hard on you and others. It demands that you stand up for it alone, including standing up for yourself — something you can do when you accept that your essential needs are met, and the others are up to you.

I have no idea how to go forward.

That could be a good thing. One clarification: While you must stand alone, you are not alone. You have help, no matter what happens.

Thank you, I think.

You're welcome. Just don't think too much.

I feel my will, but it's trembling.

Fair enough. Your part is to come open before your beloved and ask for what you need to know. Come not with what you think you know or with any kind of expectation. There are names for many things that cannot be explained. Your ability to say the names is meaningless. The names themselves are meaningless without the experience of them. So come empty to experience being filled, come with the humility to receive whatever you need, come simply with your love.

*F*loat with wordless openness into the being of all. There is nothing to fear. Even the newest or oldest dragon appearing along the way can be a gift. Under the fearsome attire is a quaking child longing to be part of the whole. Essential safety is provided. The steps are guided. Set your intent and trust.

But a sadness is sitting heavily on my chest.

The sadness—do not push it away. Expose it to the sun. It will lighten in the hands of love, from within and without. It comes from love denied, withheld, or taken away. It resonates with the cries of all mankind and the very earth upon which you walk. You can hold on to it or allow it to be transformed. Allow with an open heart. Connect with the source as best you can and trust.

Infinity has no distance either ahead or behind in time as you know it. Your focus is best put on being, receiving, allowing, offering. Let go of all concepts and concerns about how far you have come. Rather, be wholeheartedly (a wonderful word) where you are, for that is where you can be touched by the eternal. That is the only place from which transformation can happen.

As you experience the joining, all else falls away. Only you can experience how this is for you. Just be there and let go of any question, evaluation, judgment. Those are separators. From the longing of your heart, feel the pull and go with it. Your heart is all you need to take with you. Turn your back on the cries of outrage as you leave other desires behind and don't look back.

Sometimes I feel like a jumbled mixture of the best and the worst and all that lies between. Is my heart's desire strong enough?

That is for you to find out. It is the opportunity that your human life gives you—to discover the longing of your heart and let it be fulfilled.

You have kindred spirits around you, and you give much to one another. Yet, you walk alone, even as you are surrounded by so many who are lovingly lighting your way. Only you can do the walking. Sometimes even the effort to walk will do, but that effort must be yours. That is as it needs to be.

When you are in balance, you can see clearly, speak with wisdom, and walk knowingly, as clarity comes naturally to the openly receiving being. Opportunity comes as a gift. Assign no problems to it. You can be curious as to how the gift will manifest but allow no concerns about that. Obstacles that seem to tower over you menacingly are but specs upon the ground in the larger view. Stand in the place of the largest view you can attain and behold. Become a spectator to the glory that shines forth in the light. Hold the handle of the kite string and follow it up to where it flies.

Some apparent problems seem to loom over me with a cacophony of "what ifs."

What they hate most is to be ignored. Hold on to your certainty and feel the power, the love, the dominance of the power born of the joining of finite and infinite as the human soul reaches for home.

Let your life be orchestrated from spirit. Rest in the hands that so lovingly enfold you and find your peace. Receive, respond, and give out—let what is given emanate from the source through you. That is your privilege, your challenge, and your salvation.

When I feel that happening, I know it is the way I want to live. Yet it is still something of a rarity.

It is no small thing to make a total shift in the understanding of who you are and why you are here at this time. It is a shift in consciousness, which is both huge and a natural evolution. You reach out and the connection is made. You are called and you respond. You call out and your call is answered. As obstacles come up and you feel lost and alone, you must know and accept that you are not. Those are the times when you just hold on until the veil drops, and you find yourself stronger and clearer than ever. It could be called growing pains. They happen but don't have to.

Through the darkness, the light streams into you to show the way. Darkness itself becomes the backdrop for the full glory of the light that shines and transforms.

At times, I am drawn into a space of feeling, expanding, resonating, and I just want to be there. Even as awe fills me, even as I sense the power, even as I feel I am traveling through worlds, I am held within the love that I trust. Like a child with each hand securely grasped by a loving parent, I can see the wonders as they unfold, be guided through them.

A good analogy. You can trust it, for it is you, yourself unfolding. You find what you need to know as you need to know it. It keeps things simple. So many questions come. Focus on the answers and watch the questions melt away.

That which carries the water of life to you is unique to you— not the water itself but the delivery. As special as that is, the point is to drink the water. Drink deep and often. Hold on to the hands that guide you, guard you, draw you along your path of becoming until the one you were created to be becomes. Your prayer for guidance puts you in receiving mode. Understanding comes in many forms. Recognize, receive, and go forward.

How is it that I can feel the eternal in this human state of being in which my spirit walks?

You know that which many call *god* through experience. Sometimes words come, and sometimes there are none — just the feeling of being in a presence that is all you could ever want. All else can be as it may be. The path is not the destination.

You cannot resolve anything by fighting with it, by trying to interpret with your intellect. You cannot. Clarity comes from absorbing or being absorbed by something whose very being encompasses all.

I feel the truth of this but cannot grasp it.

This kind of truth cannot be grasped. The human hand, even the human mind, is a bit small to get a hold of such unlimited power and love. When you let go of your concepts and just experience it, you know with certainty.

Yes.

You experience the indefinable, not your idea of it but the actuality of it. As distractions and disturbances come, let them alert you to lock into the knowing that is unfolding, to the place where doubt does not enter, the place where peace rules.

Mary B. Gallwey

You are walking through a garden where the roses have thorns, where the perfume of beauty wafts through the stench of refuse. From east and west, north, and south, men and women of spirit have touched on the same truth and recorded it with a variety of words, encased it in a variety of conceptualizations, in their attempt to receive and take in that truth as best they can within the world in which they live.

You know what you know, and what you know, you cannot say. Focus on what you know and how you know it, not on what you don't know, which is considerable.

Listen for the call that streams into you; hear it and respond. Stark is the simplicity at the core of all things. Keep it simple, baby!

Your essential being is held in moments too small for happenings. Each moment's existence is part of a stream, flowing through time.

Yet the anxiety generated by perceived problems and possible tragic outcomes takes hold of my awareness, shutting out the light of what I know.

Fear shuts out love, and love dissolves fear. Love is not based on outcomes. It is self-powering. Only you can choose which to trust, which to fuel with your attention.

Anxiety comes, seemingly of its own accord. It doesn't knock on the door.

Maybe so, but you still have the power to choose the direction and subject of your attention, your trust. Even when you feel infused with anxiety, you can know it is ephemeral. It cannot rule you without your belief in its power.

The power of anxiety is based on the pictures of disaster it so cleverly inspires. You have the power to choose what pictures to look at, to imagine unfolding.

You underestimate your strength. So many apparent tragedies in your life have delivered new possibilities instead of the expected disaster. Don't allow yourself to play out the potential tragedy in your mind. Be strict with it, for it brings you nothing good. As you step back from frightening and challenging situations, leave room for a good outcome, for your own capacity to take one step at a time, to leave room for solutions you cannot imagine. Learn to stay in a place that allows the unexpected to emerge.

During the years of the pandemic, I allowed myself to be confined, not just physically but mentally and spiritually.

Yes, and now you are being dragged out of that state. It will serve you to add your own intention and power to the process. Experiment with the mode of being here as opposed to escaping through distractions. In your attempt to escape, you sacrifice your ability to be aware of the magic that can unfold.

The ultimate love is not a burden, for it cannot be picked up or carried. It comes to you as a gift that seeks to flow through you to wherever it needs to go. It neither belongs to you nor stays with you, any more than the air that you breathe. It continues to be fresh and renewed. This is the love born of the joining of power and compassion, strength, and serenity—each reinforced by the other. It emanates from a source that will not be defined by a name, though many names are given to it.

This love does not engender attachment, for its nature is to be freely received and freely given. It has its own rhythm, which beats individually within each one who openly receives it. And it flows outward individually through the energy and the voice of the one who, having received, purposefully allows its transmission.

Such a love cannot be contained without being distorted. It fills the receiver to overflowing, which is the point, isn't it? Find the way for it to flow through you, first by understanding that it is not yours. You are allowed to feel its reverberating beauty, to feel how it connects you to its source, and to receive its gifts to the extent that you expand for it within.

But you are only a transmission station. Understand that. Ask to understand and to be protected. It is only in trying to grab hold or direct that your own heart can be bruised. If you receive and embrace that that knowing, everything else is automatic.

How will I learn about this?

These words give you an overview and some direction. Your learning and understanding must come from experience. Ask, receive, be grateful, observe. Feel your way, and your understanding will grow, will become a part of you.

Your effort and your heart's true desire work together to hold your attention in place. Connect with them so that it is you, your will, and your love, as one, that make the choice to be single pointed.

Each distraction can either pull you away or prompt you to hold on tighter. It is all a matter of timely recognition, identifying distraction for what it is before it gains a hold on your attention. Feel free to ask for help. Help waits upon your request.

I feel so inadequate.

But you are not the judge of that. Insecurity about your worth is a dangerous under-miner and a poor excuse. Do not allow it. As a human being, you have a potential that you have yet to explore fully. Do you want to explore it?

Yes.

Then all you have to do is keep on trekking. You will learn and discover. The school is challenging, but life itself becomes the very best tutor to help further your understanding of the knowing, the gift, that flows into you.

The path of each individual is unique. Each has its own challenges. When a sauce is poured onto the surface of a sponge cake, it takes some time to soak through. Each time one layer is saturated, there is another. As long as your intention is clear, you can trust the process.

It is through love that the integration of time and timelessness happens. Love is both the guide and the fulfillment, the uniter. It has the unique power to mend the lover and the one loved on all levels—the ultimate one being union with the Whole, evolving in degrees, moving toward and away through time until time itself dissolves.

So where does that leave me in this life with all its circumstances and variables?

It leaves you as a traveler who is free to choose the map you will use to proceed on the journey it makes. Typical pathways are circuitous or more direct depending on the motivation of the traveler. The wise one consults the map often, remembers the purpose behind the chosen direction, and observes the wanderings off the path, which is generally full of misleading distractions.

That brings up an important question that needs resolution. Distraction is a strategy used to avoid negative or threatening emotions, providing some illusion of safety.

But safety does not emerge from distraction or disconnection. It is strengthened in the stages the union with the whole that is independent of circumstances, which are always temporary in the long view.

Love is your vehicle, the engine that propels you forward. Like any vehicle, it needs attention, nurturing, exploration, discovery, and most of all, the freedom to shine out to other forms of life.

Take the time to digest this and see where it leads you. Discover Love, distinguish it from sentiment, from ego-based emotion. So back to the question: Does your focus hone in on self-protection or on trusting the journey and its destination?

When your childhood terror was first dissolved, it was with the power of Love, and you saw that clearly. What is received so abundantly needs to go out through you or it will stagnate. It can be a self-driving vehicle if allowed its freedom.

Your life adventure is to discover what that would entail, what it would look like. It is very individual at the start and may not look like you imagine it should. The knowing of it does not come through logic or words. It is designed to unfold in response to the deep-seated desire of the eternal heart.

And yet here are words.

Just hints, clues for the treasure hunt, for your understanding is still furthered by words that you cannot ultimately define with your brain. Signposts at best. The heart has been caged. Can you set the lion free? It may look risky.

It seems like the ultimate challenge.

One of them.

Fear is my earliest remembered emotion.

Yes. What is your earliest remembered feeling?

The total security of being held in my mother's arms. A feeling held onto by sucking my thumb.

Mm. An effective method of shutting out the threats of the unknown or the fearsome. Want to find another one? It is receiving and giving, in and out like breath—a very natural process that has been obscured by all that is unnatural and contrived.

Here is a hint. Start with the first received and recognized love. The eternal one, that you experienced firsthand as a young child. It hasn't gone anywhere, and it knows the way. You don't have to. Actually, it is best if you accept that you don't know the way. Just be alert for the simple revelations as they come.

How strange it is to go into that unfathomable space of union, freedom, and surrendering to the shower of bliss so it may be whatever it is at that moment and then come back to do taxes! How can it be? How can I be in tax mode without letting go of that other space of being?

You are part of the eternal movement of spirit integrating with the world of physical form. Though the references to that are many, you cannot imagine how it will come to be, much less how it is coming to be now. If you desire to participate in that, then all you do can be part of it. You are no longer separate. It's just that you have a way of forgetting, falling back into the belief that you are on your own, alone.

Embrace the unity, not just when you are in a profound state of focus within your spirit but also as you meet up with and take on the everyday tasks of your life. Whether it is sweeping a floor, enjoying a meal, listening to a friend, or going about "earning a living"—such a very strange phrase! — you are equipped to bring your awareness and intended responsiveness along with you.

The same possibility of seeing, feeling, and allowing the power to come through you in its chosen way is always there. Moments of experience are not limited by physical or even mental actions unless you fail to see that possibility.

Why would the being of love warm you through and through only to toss you out into the cold? That's not how it is. You can bring the radiating cloak of warmth with you so that its light may expand who you are and what you have to give any time you let it. Stop thinking, you know which actions are important and which are not. It is not the actions but the being you bring to them that matters. You have a great variety of situations to practice with.

Remember that feeling of letting go with trust. Then bring it into your actions as you apply your energy, intelligence, and intuitive choices to your daily life. Getting out of the judgment seat has meaning you haven't yet fully grasped. You are not in a position to judge which individual people or events are good or bad, any more than you can judge the state of the world as a whole. And that's because you cannot see either people or events or the world as a whole. You just see random pieces.

Assessing happens from a different kind of awareness than judging. Assessment is not predisposed. It is the result of conscious, objective observation, and it is an important skill to develop both for your safety and your effectiveness. It can be based on intuition, facts, or both. By nature, it is free of emotion and self-serving ambition. When judgment, anticipation, expectation, and egocentricity fade, freedom, joy, and usefulness replace them.

It sounds so simple.

That's because it is. Simple can still be challenging. Try it and see how it goes. It's a dare!

Moments of feeling whole and undivided descend upon me like an awakening rain, and I feel them with amazement, wonder.

What you long for is manifesting for you even though you do not know exactly what it is. When you feel what seems like such undeserved kindness filling your experience of being, it is natural to feel both gratitude and a compelling longing for more. It is the very satisfaction of that desire that uncovers or makes room for more. What used to satisfy no longer does. It's a bit relentless.

Unimaginable love awaits the open heart. Leave no room for doubt. Even when you feel you are walking blind, you have help. Even when you feel lost, you can make the effort to be found. This way of being overcomes fear, boredom, anxiety—dissatisfaction of any kind—for it shares no space with any of them.

Being in such a place of recognition is all that is of consequence for you. So, you can forget the pecking order that you have been taught. You are often incapable of knowing what is or isn't important in your reasoning mind or your emotions because you engage with such a small fraction of the whole.

You know by staying connected to the place of knowing that is becoming more real for you. That is your lifeline in more ways than one.

Of primary importance is your consciousness—what you are tuned in to—for that is what instructs your responses to the changes in the ever-changing world in which you physically live.

I see all the failures and hear the voice of recrimination, but what I feel is the love showering over me with a protective force. It puzzles me, for I am trained to feel I need to deserve to be loved. Only the sheer pleasure of this grace and the longing it elicits undermines the foundation of training, habit, flawed conclusions.

There is a lot here for you, child of many years. You cannot deserve and you cannot lose this love that needs only your openness to fill you. You can only pull away from it into the world where you imagine more control. But that's not what you are doing. You are falling in love with the love, and you return to it persistently. You are allowing yourself to see, to observe the distractions, and to try again. Just get out of the judgment seat.

You will come back to that consciousness you seek countless times before you can stay in it. You are learning to walk. You are learning to trust, and it still feels like a risky business at times. You see and feel perceived threats and want to hide under the covers. One day you will know the "boogeyman" for what it is and be able to open the closet doors to find it monster-free with your own light.

That's an image that causes quivering in my stomach and utter longing in my heart, and I think my soul as well.

Yes. It is the human propensity to see the ultimate security as a risk. Do you want to be motivated by fear or love? If it is the latter, all you need to do is let go the imaginings and hold on to the true. How do you know the true? It is the one thing that you know with certainty when you feel it. It may be inexplicable, but it is utterly recognizable to the sincere heart. Each moment of recognition builds your foundation.

Why not forget the idea of deserving and cling to the love you are showered with? It is the love that draws your attention and your gratitude that holds it. Effort, too, but that comes out of intention, and intention is born in your heart out of your own love. It is when your love meets the love that the opening happens for you. The receiver gives and the giver receives in the unfathomable mystery of union; then love reigns in utter majesty.

I turn again and again to the bliss of simple being and am rescued from the abyss of fear and uncertainty. Then when someone asks how I am doing, my attention goes to the struggle as though to convey how well I am doing despite how things are. Valiant me! And for that moment of perceived glory, I give it away, let go of the reigning beauty. Something there is that is attached to suffering, hesitant to embrace the perfection, the song of a life in synch with its own tune. ACCEPTANCE. What a hugely encompassing word.

Let yourself be happy—plain and simple—not despite this or that. Just happy. Stay in the embrace, open to the love. *Receive.*

Gentle hands caress a yearning spirit,

Whispering the way

With the softness of a subtle breeze,

Heard only in the stillness of receiving.

*I*n gifted moments I am absorbed into the vastness of simple being — dissolved and expanded, and then.... Yes, the "then" of the world of time reemerges, threatens to take me away into its realm of separation.

The one is with you in the world of many. Will you hold on or separate? This is the choice made in milliseconds, often passing unobserved. The observer — the I that you are — led by its longing, becomes ever more aware of the little things that erode the balance, the wholeness of being. These "little things" are like termites feasting on the structure of a house, your house.

Always there is the question: What do you want? Will you choose from a place of awareness or oblivion? The key is attention. You can work on that all day long, no matter what you are "doing." One focus, one motive, perpetuated by your own decision, provides a dome of consciousness arching over all that exists in your world and the worlds beyond. The cry of your heart emerges from its deepest desire until it determines your thoughts and actions. There is a homing device deep in your heart. Listen for it.

There is a thread of light stronger than any rope of steel between you and your heart's desire, your destination. Trust it. It is connected with your reason for being where and who you are. Sometimes you resist being both where you are and who you are, at least potentially. From that resistance comes pain, anxiety, tension, and breakdown.

Of all the things you think you can't afford; those are the primary ones. Hold on to all you know that is good, and you will slowly find the secret of compassion coming from strength, from clarity. You will learn how to proceed without being drawn away from your own thread of light. You will learn to stand in that light, shielded by it and enlightened by it. So very much to discover and make your own. Let your desire for the eternal be your guide.

The path to your destination is the fulfillment of your desire. The map for the journey is laid out through all the moments of your day. Remember that. You need a flashlight or flash of light to see it. Three words from this missive turn it on: Listen, Trust, and Remember. You are never alone; however, you are feeling. Furthermore, you have an agreement to fulfill.

From the time we are born into a human body, the improvement program begins. It is first imposed most well-meaningly by our parents or caretakers who are not familiar with just loving what is and taking care of obvious needs. That would involve acceptance of a new being and caring to provide that tiny baby a nest to grow in naturally with curiosity to learn. But that runs counter to your culture, almost every culture, actually.

We are always trying to improve on what is instead of seeing its uniqueness. The point is to support your natural growth, understanding, and independence, not to shape it into our idea of someone extraordinary. Soon you yield to self-judgement, measuring yourself against the societal standard, and beginning to be ruled by the thoughts of what is good and what is bad, by what brings approval. That is the beginning of a lifetime struggle. We see ourselves in comparison to others and miss who we uniquely are.

As this pattern repeats in millions of individual forms, the core of the individual is wounded, undermined. Each one develops their own methods of protecting against these wounds. Some of them get buried deep. Some get redefined into something acceptable. Some are simply set aside and ignored.

So, what is to be done? What are the options for each misshapen individual? It involves a journey into the core self, the original one that took its first breath before the onslaught began, however well-meaning. Then with tremendous courage, it takes acceptance without judgement or comparisons—that very acceptance that the newborn so deeply needed. Be careful here. This acceptance is entirely free of judgement.

It opens a space for the wonder of discovery of a unique, truly one-of-a-kind, living, individual—undivided. This person may be aware of being on a journey, and on that journey may make choices that eventually determine the final destination. But what will guide those choices? Will it be the grid of comparisons and standards imposed by society? Or will it be a connection with the untarnished self that longs for its own fulfillment?

That self knows what releases joy, freedom, and unhampered growth. That self is precious. There is a learning curve ahead of it, mostly involving the shedding of illusion and acceptance of being where and how it is without comparisons. It involves letting go of self-imposed boundaries, be they placed by ambition or fear, and seeing that they are not needed.

What does it take? Trust, clarity about the goal, courage to be unlike anyone else, will to keep on going, and holding on to one's own connection to that which IS always. No easy pathway, true. Yet there is no more direct one to all that the unique person that you are longs for. And it is so very rewarding.

Don't wait to know how to begin. Just begin, and the way will open itself before you. As you get to know the I that you are, the chains fall off one by one as long as you leave behind any picture of that idealized I of your own making. Let it be, let it discover, let it grow into a manifestation of itself.

Still, I have no idea how to begin.

Perfect! That is always the best place from which to start. You are loved. A good beginning is to ask for help. Remember that one?

The doings you choose are not what is important. It is the being you embrace that determines the extent of the opening, the intention, or the attention you bring in. Those are the door openers, and each door you go through leads to another. This is not a finite journey. So, measuring where you are on it is somewhat ridiculous. After all, what is 50% of infinity?

So just begin and then begin again and again. Hold your being in a moment too small for happenings. The moment's existence is part of a stream, flowing through time.

Yet the anxiety empowered by perceived problems and possibly tragic outcomes takes hold of my awareness, shutting out the light of my inner knowing.

Fear shuts out love and love dissolves fear. Love is not based on outcomes. It is self-powering. Only you can choose which to trust, which to fuel with your attention.

The anxiety comes, seemingly of its own accord. It doesn't knock on the door.

Maybe so, but you still have the power to choose the direction and subject of your attention, your trust. Even when you feel infused with anxiety, you can know it is ephemeral. It cannot rule you without your belief in its power. The power of anxiety is based on the pictures of disaster it so cleverly inspires. You get to choose what pictures to look at, to imagine unfolding.

You underestimate your strength. So many apparent tragedies in your life have delivered new possibilities instead of the expected disaster. Don't allow yourself to play out the potential tragedy in your mind. Be strict with it, for it brings you no good. As you step back from frightening and challenging situations, leave room for a good outcome, for your own capacity to take one step at a time, to leave room for solutions you cannot imagine. Learn to be in a place that allows the unexpected to emerge.

I have been in lockdown mode for a couple of years, allowing myself to be confined, not just physically but mentally and spiritually.

Yes, and now you are being dragged out of that state. It will serve you to add your own intention and power to the process. Experiment with the mode of being here as opposed to escaping through distractions. In doing so, you sacrifice your ability to be aware of the magic that can unfold.

As I begin to understand my smallness, I begin to step through the cracks in time, to be absorbed by the infinite. The oneness of all erases ego even as it enhances the power that can emanate from the source of my existence—the power of the humble soul that has lost the desire to possess it.

The vastness is stunning until I disappear into it in gifted spans of timelessness while still inhabiting a body. Even as my consciousness settles back into the time-bound cadence of this life, I have the opportunity to continue knowing the oneness.

In the experience of oneness, you find the ultimate place of balance between all the opposites. It is a point of neutrality, of wholeness, that allows untainted observation. In that connective state, you stand fearless, a tool of both destruction and creation, as both are part of the pathway of life.

Learn to live in the neutral point of balance between emotion and rationality, expansion and contraction, bondage, and abandon. This is the origin of true freedom from the bonds of your limited human understanding to unfettered seeing, hearing, and knowing. It is from this state of balance that you can truly serve the oneness you are a part of, free of the limitations of judgment.

Once you see this truth, you can begin the work of integrating, of merging previously separate worlds of ever-changing form and eternal spirit, of time and eternity. The learning involved is arduous, sometimes awkward, even repugnant. It involves the constant recognition and reformation of ingrained habit with the inner power of will and persistence until the experience of effortlessness is reached and a new normal is established. The resistance it evokes along the way holds the key to understanding what holds you back.

This journey is as relentless as it is rewarding, made alone in one sense but also in step with kindred spirits both known and unknown. The aloneness lies only in the necessity of individual choice. That remains sacrosanct. So, while you make your choices alone, you are not alone. You are already part of the oneness that has always been.

Awareness of inner strengths, of the inner heart of peace, illuminates the power of choice. In the field of choice, the battle begins between the longing of the heart and the lure of apartness with its minions of fear, greed, and the false promise of control. The first seems risk-filled but offers stability, creativity, and joy. The second seems stable but offers disintegration and destruction in the long run.

CHOICE leaves life direction in the hands of the individual. What will motivate the choices that chart the course of a life? Attention and awareness within the moments of the stream of life. Attention is fueled by will and consciousness. The stream of one life and its myriad of choices, often conflicting, is but a tiny part of the stream of ongoing life.

Along this journey, the choices do not demand loss of control of attention and motive. It just requires an understanding of what the individual does not have effective control over, what happens in the cycles of existence around us.

I recognize that I don't know what I need, despite thinking I do. Still, what I actually need is provided flawlessly. It is for me to recognize and appreciate that.

The place of attentive anticipation is full of the openness of a free heart.

Questions lead to further learning. Doubts shut down the clear observation that leads to learning, to knowing. Doubts, like termites, bore into the structure of one's being and gnaw away at it relentlessly.

Look closely at the doubts when they appear so as to distinguish them from questions. Questions powered by the desire to know require unbiased observation, which in turn, is free to come to conclusions about the matter on hand. Many questions lead to further questions. They may lead to the rejection of a belief, a theory, or a possibility. Doubt tends to undermine the ability to see clearly. It closes doors so that the conclusions they lead to have a flimsy basis.

You are born with the instinct to know your world and all its goings on. Just watch a baby move beyond the instinct to survive into a state of constant observation as that new life sorts out the people and things, body senses, and the innate distinction between comfort and discomfort, contentment, and pain, slowly being shaped by experience.

Remember that each moment is new even as you categorize it in a stream with a label. The observer in you is curious to see the reality of what it is focused on. It is quick to recognize hidden beauty amidst what appears ugly or threatening.

Add the kindling of your recognition of that hidden beauty and it begins to manifest, to spread, to emerge from its own dark corner. As every artist knows, darkness and shadow are needed to expose the reality of the images. So, it is with our own darkness.

Along the Way

The way ahead is easy because it is natural. It is hard because it is still unfamiliar and somewhat uncommon—a road less traveled for sure. It won't fit into any of your ideas about it. What is "it"? It is something that has been destroyed again and again by people's need to define everything, to bring things down to a manageable size. Cultures and belief systems of all kinds have provided a prison for the free spirit should one feel the need for that.

Explore the naturalness that fills you with the vibrancy of life in motion with a quiet mind that is free to see what it is. Enjoy both what you know and what you don't know.

Your concern right now is not the system of any teaching but submerging yourself in what your learning reveals. You cannot catch a moment, but you can fly with it through the stream of one to another, remaining in the presence.

In the darkness shines the glory of light if you have the eyes for it, even within a seemingly darkening world.

Part Three

Peace is the province of each individual, not of countries or leaders squabbling over perceived advantages, be they sources of wealth or the power of ideas. Within each person is the gloriousness of a living, vibrating, expanding peace, and for each one it is a life's work, often a struggle, to live in it, to know it, to become one with it.

Your habitual shield of protection against the threats that abound around you, even within you, is to fend them off with diversions. It is a way of ignoring their existence, and it's not a bad strategy. Much better than giving such perceived threats the power of your belief in their power, for that only gives them strength.

Slowly, you will learn the strategy of embracing your own power, or more accurately, the power of spirit that dwells within you, and trusting it. Find your freedom in the trust of that power. Let that be how you use the energy of your life. Listen, for you are being taught. The course is open and free to all who want to take it. It is tough and demanding, but the only failure is that of dropping out.

Seeing is not believing, you know; experiencing is. Recognize the feeling of the true and let it manifest without limitation. Whether it is many with one voice or one with many voices, is immaterial. Just listen and hear; receive and learn; grow and enjoy what evolves. Like a child first learning the alphabet, you cannot foresee what will come out of understanding how the letters work together to bring forth meaning. Stay with it, and you will witness "the peace that passes all understanding" fear.

By the way, where dangers are real, it is wise to be intelligent about them. Precautions are in order, just not unharnessed.

There is a you that has lived many lives, and it is that you that longs to be in sync with its source, to serve a greater purpose. So, you could say that you have to get out of this particular life's drama, disentangle yourself, so that it is the very essence of you that offers, or more aptly, requests to serve.

It is in the essence of that distilled you that you can even begin to understand, to feel the purity of this desire, untainted by others. Then in this particular life, you can view the vast variety of conditions that you may act upon, or not. Both the request and the commitment come from your spirit, while the enactment and the learning play out in the day-to-day or moment-to-moment flow of your life now.

It is a continuous cycle of finding the perspective, the feeling, the heart of the one purpose, and bringing it down to the world of many as best you can, again and again and again. To do that you have to accept that from within the battle, no matter what the fight or struggle is, you cannot see the solution, the way to resolution or to peace. You need access to a different perspective.

Move out of the battlefield to find your guiding principle, and when you have it, let it be your guide. The guiding principle for each situation emerges from the place where there is no doubt, no argument, no human emotions—just the stark clarity of the observer.

You find this principle, or as much of it as you can grasp, for yourself alone. You can speak of it to others, but you have no say and no stake in how much of it they will see. Those who are truly dedicated to the same goals will find unity through it, though maybe not immediately.

We all have our obstacles—the things we want or feel we need, the things we hold on to that may not be in line with the larger view. Your own battles are enough to be involved with. Even those people you are closest to have theirs that you do not share.

So, as you interact with others, keep your eye on your best understanding of your highest purpose and let go of everything else. Listen for your words of wisdom but let them fall on others' ears however they do. Listen again and let the words or actions come through you from that unique place of unbiased observation.

You are not the judge of results, although you may sometimes be a witness to them, from one point of view. The only stake you have is in your own response and the place of being from which you make it. That is your work. All others have their own.

Listen, respond, and observe until you are done. Then disengage and let go of the issue, whatever it is. If you do not, you will inevitably be pulled into another seductive tangle, and more the fool are you.

There is such a grace and flow to the movements and thoughts that stem from unity with the eternal. There is the feeling of great purpose, and that purpose is the unity itself. In the moments of embracing that, there is focus without effort; there is effort without strain; and the feeling of oneness itself is all there is to gain.

All the situations in life are but the practice field upon which the soul spins the fragments of its redemption. Over time, each fragment can be woven into a complete garment worthy of the wedding, the joining, of this one of many with that which is one.

Treasure these moments and let them imprint themselves upon your experience that you may learn to extend them along the timeline of this life that you are living. Each moment of unity is a door to infinity.

What is it that stands in the way? What is it that erodes your intention, erodes your very foundation? The answer to be discovered personally by each soul lies in the ongoing struggle between the forces that vie for control—control of a moment, an individual, or of humankind as a whole. This battleground lies within you.

One side works with illusion—the concept or imagination of what will satisfy, what will give this human being some say over destiny. It thrives in the perspective of the immediate—of short-term gain, of whatever satisfies the endless desires of the base soul.

The other side offers paradoxes: freedom out of servitude, receiving out of giving, expansion out of single pointedness. It manifests in the now, eluding the bonds of time.

You stand in the middle of the field with a very powerful weapon—the right of choice made repeatedly until it is fulfilled. Conscious choice, whether it appears big or small, requires effort both in the making and the follow through. And that effort triggers the most unexpectedly delightful support—playful, light, powerful, and so very attractive.

Your life is an opportunity to learn to hold to your primary choice. Sometimes doing so seems to require the willingness to sacrifice. Yet in the long run, this seeming sacrifice is but the doorway to your fulfillment—something you might call joy, peace, or contentment though they are only elements of it.

There are endless ways in which you can allow yourself to be overtaken by the undermining search for perceived personal power or gratification. And there are endless opportunities to allow your moments to unfold consciously. This is the effort to become what you are—not just for now but for always—in the place or space where measured time dissolves into the timeless and life is indeed eternal.

Think about these things and let your growing understanding inform your actions and your choices. It is a learning that is never static or complete. It evolves continually, revealing new horizons along with new challenges. That is the essential difference between a belief system and the path of the constantly evolving human soul, the path that leads home.

The moments of life are precious and, of course, limited in the world of time. The enjoyment of them, even the awareness of them, is often shadowed by anxiety, anger, dilemmas, and problems of an infinite variety. This is the way it is for most members of humankind. Even "positive" emotions can take over the simple gift of awareness.

Emotions, drives, and needs are part of human life. And all add to the potential progression of understanding and balance if one ingredient remains active: awareness of the constant gift of life itself.

What is that gift? It cannot be defined, but on Earth only humans have the ability to see it. It is the capacity to see beyond immediate reactions and connect with that which exists outside of time, even as time affects all things in human life. In the space of that recognition, a connection is made that reveals that there is always a way forward and the opportunity to discover it.

The things we struggle with change in their nature, in their effect on us, when the "light" switch is on, and we can see through the darkness. What does it take to see beyond present concerns, drives, and emotions? It is nothing less than consciousness and connection with that which is not bound by time. The way forward is seen differently in that mode. It is like an oxygen mask that delivers clean air to a firefighter. We are all fighting fires or trying to avoid them. Not so enjoyable.

Let go of the burdens long enough to see past them. Unimagined solutions await that step as does profound enjoyment and safety. Think about what you know and what you don't know. You will never know what the future, even the immediate one, can bring. Yet you have the capacity to know of something you can experience, something that remains in place even when you ignore it. It has no name but is always present.

The challenge to break through the patterns absorbed since birth, to become free of them, is one of *the* greatest, if not the greatest, you will meet in this life. The reward is potentially the greatest as well. It does not happen speedily, but in small moments of time seeded by understanding and growing desire. As you want it, it shall evolve like a seedling well-tended. The essential nourishment of its growth is love, the one in your heart mingling with the eternal one from which you sprang.

The personality-based ego wants credit for what is deemed good by others and to be blameless for what is deemed bad. But there is confusion for most about what is the I that is you. There is an I that is the one that can choose what to listen to, where to turn, what to strive for. That is the one that can raise its consciousness, that can feel the voice of the infinite, be fed by it, be led by it. That is the I who determines what to trust.

So where is this I going to place any credit or offer trust? In whose hands will it entrust its well-being? Does it choose to associate with the credit monger whose very substance is illusory? Or does it seek cleansing from that which has never broken the trust?

Along the Way

There is no need to fear the exploration of the dark places, for therein lies the beginning of healing. It is part of the dance of redemption, during which the loved is drawn to the lover and finite surrenders to infinite in a stream of life-changing moments. The power retained is that of choice until that choice is complete.

In the simplicity of how it is, the demands of the ego give way to the power of love each time the heart stays true, each time it even pleads for the strength to stay true, along this journey through time.

Of the many desires, wants, attractions, preferences, which ones will become the foundation of your intentions and the motivation of your actions? To even see that choice, much less to make it, it is best to be removed from the turmoil to a place where you can both see and feel your priority—that one ordering goal that you set for this life.

When you receive, accept. Consciously take in the gift of love that is flowing to you, and it can go out from you to others. You cannot achieve love. You can only welcome it, allow it to do its work within you, appreciate it, and let it come through you uncontaminated. It is a most natural process.

The love that you have sought so anxiously all your life is yours. You have it already—highest quality, immaculate, pure from the source with countless facets that reflect out in different ways, from one into many and from many back to one.

It is your privilege to feel the magic and watch it unfold. In your freedom, you become the observer of utter magnificence.

The great shifter of understanding comes with your realization that there is a purpose for being who and where you are. Your instincts of preservation tell you at best an incomplete story. Self-preservation but of what self? There is for each one an eternal self that is part of the ongoing creation of the power that first brought form into being. That creation, that healing of souls, the very light of spirit, is still evolving.

When you doubt, do you know what you are doubting? You are doubting your source self, your eternal self. Is that too much to accept? Within that acceptance is all the calm you need in the storm, in any storm that comes. And storms will come, just as sunny days—both inner and outer.

You get frustrated when your plans don't work out, when you feel thwarted in what you want or feel you need in the immediate circumstances of your daily life. Step back. Whatever you do, wherever you go, whatever your conditions or situations, the living power of love and wisdom can shine through you to others in ways you may never know.

That is the possibility of each soul, but how many know it?

What it takes to make this journey of soul is no less than everything. What is received in return is no less than everything, to the extent you can be open to it. What this means is only just dawning on you with the first flickers of the light of the sun glowing upon your horizon. You have no need or ability to make the sun rise. Just appreciate it. Absorb its life-giving rays and remember that no life exists without it.

Your lamp has been lit; protect its flame first of all. Lay down other concerns in deference to that one concern, and you will find your way through all the others. You will know what you need to know, when you need to know it, and any needed action on your part will manifest toward the intended end. That is the ultimate promise life offers to you and to all mankind.

*T*hen you are the recipient of the love that fills you, that melts all your boundaries of separation, that folds its arms around you until all your troubles and concerns are dissolved, you just want to remain in that experience. Yet you are living in a world of form and motion, of people and things interacting. You are part of that world and choose what part to play in it moment by moment.

The innate response to receiving love that asks nothing back is to return it however you can. It becomes a need, and that need becomes an opportunity to serve that which no name describes.

When a guileless soul longs to return the growing love inspired—literally breathed in—that soul seeks understanding beyond its capacity, and that understanding evolves. Understanding expands as long as it is welcomed and the choice to exercise it is ongoing.

The one who chooses to give to others in this way often does so without even knowing it. The energy of the eternal giver simply flows through such a person. When they are aware of it, they receive even more than they could ever hope to give.

This dance of love between a soul and its source is totally individual. It is like a snowflake that, while it is easily recognized as a snowflake, is never replicated. The design is unique, as is each human being.

If you desire to serve, first know that you do not know how. Ask and you will discover, according to your capacity and openness. It takes great humility always. It takes clarity of intention, sincerity of motive, and focus of attention. With that, the one you were born to be can manifest its own uniqueness and beauty along its way through this life. You can come into your own, truly be yourself.

Such a freedom awaits you as you let go of how you think things should be—need to be—for your own wellbeing. As you immerse yourself in the tasks of managing the unmanageable, you take on a huge burden. You become driven by the need to personally see that everything turns out well, or at least as you envision "well" to be.

So, you take on the impossible with valiant energy, forcing your way toward the satisfaction of perceived needs. Let go! Listen in silence to the knower within you. Remember the end goal. Remember that it is often hard to know which station along the way is actually taking you closer to where you want to go.

You live in a world of illusion. What seems like a really good thing may lead to a dead end. What seems like a bad thing can be transformed into a secret passageway to what you seek in your heart of hearts.

Step back as each day begins and remember the end goal— the one you have chosen consciously or unconsciously for your life. Let that remembrance refresh your perspective, remind you of what you know and what you don't know.

You struggle with this. What does it all mean? These are words for the ones who want to be in tune with the source of life everlasting, who want above all to be available for that energy to flow through them.

Wake up and see your day and all that appears to be part of it, and then leave room for the unforeseeable. Lay down the burdens, the "have tos"; listen to the music of the great musician, the creator of the symphony, and to the notes you are invited to play. Trust and then let your effort flow like a river, scrambling over obstacles with a relentlessness masked as gay abandon. Enjoy. Feel the power and the lightness of the light that is at once your guide and your destination.

When you are feeling connected with presence, there is no peril except that of letting go of it. You know that, but you must trust your knowing. The eternal has a seat within you, yet it yields to your will so that you have the chance to recognize its magnificence and embrace it with all that you are.

Rough times are ahead for your world. The need to be steadfast is urgent. In fact, it is urgent in all times. In times of challenge, you may see the truth of what you want and where your satisfaction comes from even more clearly. Value that opportunity for it will serve you.

Remember again what you know and what you do not know. You know enough of the one of all to want to be with that, to be of that, to serve that. What you don't know is which apparent losses are gifts in disguise. So be afraid, but only of one thing—letting go of your connection to that one.

Let all your affairs be guided by that single understanding. Do the work of holding on, and all shall be given. So, fear and fear not. Allow the power and the love to flow through you.

That is the greatest gift you can be offered, and it can be given in any and all circumstances. The grace is abundantly there.

There is nothing to give up except your belief that anything else matters more. This is the priceless pearl of wisdom that must be your very foundation. As you stand on that foundation, the way will be lit for you, and you will walk on it in utter safety, even through your death.

So, dear soul, lighten up! Embrace whatever is before you.

When there are serious problems or perceptions of such, the characteristic human response is to get entwined with them, mentally and emotionally. The person with the "problem" is incapacitated by them, losing the distance that would provide any chance of finding solutions.

It is best to stand back from the perceived threats that problems present as inevitable. You need a ground to stand on that lies outside the turmoil, where you can see clearly and seek your response with a calm mind.

Often problems even lead to new opportunities but not if they crowd the space where you can understand that while you are perplexed, you are not threatened from the long view. The place of safety is a place of consciousness within which you are removed from the threat, can find a longer-term perspective, and access your strengths.

You have that capacity. The first step is to take back your power-the power of the long-term view, the long-term purpose for your lifetime. Find your compassion, trust in your undisturbed insight, the grace that has shadowed you all your life.

Find your place in the situation, which is always unique. It is not one of confrontation, reaction, anger, or fear. It is one of clarity, love, and inner knowing.

*Y*ou are where you are for a reason, or actually for many reasons. Some are the results of your own choices, whether actions or inactions. Yet all offer you the opportunity to give, to learn, to advance. The steps are here, right in the complex of situations you are living in. Look for those steps, and you will see amazing things unfold. See and act from that understanding and witness the magic of the majesty of the eternal in action.

The universe does not revolve around you. You revolve within the universe as a tiny cog in the infinite realm of all that is—a cog with free will. No human being would design such a thing! How could it work? The answer to that you can only sense, for it is beyond the grasp of your human brain, however intelligent it may be. In the short run it would seem that it often doesn't work. "Working" involves the evolution of all the elements of creation into their ideal state by their own choice, attraction, and will. It is a grand drama playing out in moments and eons.

As you attempt to even image the vastness of which you are a part, you may find yourself both humbled and enlightened— able to see from a higher perspective the role you could play, the significance of what is around you, and the supreme importance of maintaining your awareness of the source of all this vastness at work as you make your way through the moments of your days.

If you are listening to this message, you are ready to do that, to keep in that level of awareness or consciousness. Respond, if that is what you want, with an open mind. Acknowledge what you don't know, which is huge, and hold on to what you do know, which is all that matters at any one point in time. Give reign to the intent with which you came, and you will surely find your way bit by bit.

Sometimes there are backward steps in the forward movement, but there don't have to be. When there are, take advantage of the learning and clarification that they offer.

As long as you are alive on this earth, there will be more to learn, to experience, to give. It is a journey to a destination you will only fully know when you get there. There will be hard times filled with obstacles, requiring great effort of will to keep going on your chosen path. There will also be flowing times when you are sailing, as down a river on a sunny day. Times of high joy seeing the vistas from the mountain top and times of desperation when you will feel as though you are trapped with no hope of release — and everything in between.

What will be your goal and what will be your guide? Both are there, lodged in your innermost knowing, waiting only for your recognition, your embrace. Your essential spirit, the core of your very being, cannot be forced. It may not have power over others, but it is endowed with authority its own actions and reactions, both internal and external.

It is in the silence of effervescent peace, of oneness, that you will find your way, your protection, and your direction. In that silence you find your strength, your courage, and your knowing. It is a gift to the open heart, to the one who asks for it with sincerity. It is in the silence that what you need to know unfolds for you, reveals itself to you.

In the silence you fall in love with the freedom of simple being as the bindings of time are loosened and the high ecstasy of unrestricted love absorbs you in its endlessness until you return to your world of time and particulars with hidden wounds majestically healed, confusions cleared, intention renewed. Such is your road, your possibility, oh fortunate one. Honor it with the way you walk through all that comes before you along the way.

*Y*ou live in a world in which it has become impossible to figure out how things will turn out. It has become too intertwined, too complex. Added to that, the forces of nature are becoming more violent and less predictable. Yet even as the activity becomes more and more futile, people everywhere are intent in plotting to force situations and outcomes to their advantage.

The wise ones, as few as they are, step back long enough to realize that such effort is wasted, at least in the long run. In stepping back, they come to understand more and more about what is actually to their advantage. They step back even further to examine their purpose in being alive at this time in the first place. They ask, "Why am I here? What do I want most of all? What is the jewel beyond price?"

Those are the individuals who truly hold outcomes in their hands because they are willing to be channels instead of players and manipulators. They at least attempt to see the larger view that cannot be seen fully from within a human body but that encompasses the destiny of man and all that exists.

The happenings are like new puzzles for you, new opportunities to take your seeing and your understanding beyond immediate appearances, to hang on to the essence of your original purpose and take your course from that. A magician works by misdirection. A puzzle is designed to camouflage the pathway to the solution. To solve it, you must notice what can only be seen from a place of objectivity, a place of apart, where you are not drawn into the plot and its false clues.

You must not fall for what looks obvious. Look deeper into the core. See your motives in the light of your primary intent and align them accordingly. Begin to see how your life purpose could be expressed or furthered in the situation at hand. You will be amazed at how freeing that is.

One of the hardest things for human beings is to find the freedom to let go of the immediate end result in favor of the ultimate one that they can sense but not fully envision. So, we get stuck in the illusion that if we can make this or that happen in a certain way, we will be further along in reaching our goal. But which goal?

When you feel driven, think about who or what is the driver. The phrase implies that you are being controlled by something other than yourself. There is civil war going on within you in which civility is usually the first casualty. Lower self meets higher self with great force. Higher self holds secure in a place away from the battle. You, the human being, must go to the solitude of the higher self to set your path—if not the how, then the direction—and aim yourself well before moving into, and hopefully through, the fray.

The control you have in your life, the arena in which you have choice, is only over yourself. It is a choice of what you will serve. When that is your sincere effort, obstacles dissolve. More than that, you will walk the path of your destiny and play a part in the unfolding of world destiny in ways you may never see. Such is the path of the humble servant. Freedom is a letting go of the many while holding on to the one.

You are where you are because you need to be there, but there is nothing about it that is necessarily restraining. Perfection awaits you. It is pure longing that takes you there. This is a time of sorting out, pulling the beautiful out of the swamp into its rightful home.

Appreciate the immaculate care you are given and trust as you make your journey homeward. Learn to see the possibility of learning and growing in each moment, each circumstance, and each condition. Your choices are made in moments, so often without your even noticing.

Allow your understanding to expand beyond the limits of intellect into the state where the truth of how it is can manifest within you. Expansion needs space, not containers.

One purpose, one direction, one destination — one love.

As you come to a new challenge, and there will be many, step back. Come to the quiet place where you can hear and understand how to respond, where you can see what your role is. Remember that the work is not yours to manage, no matter how involved you feel with it. Let what is given come through you untouched. You may be pleasantly surprised at the ease and freedom that come with this effort to stay connected and allow your higher knowing to take charge. In that place of connection, you are free from fear, need, emotional snags, history, and habit.

In the place of ultimate understanding, there are no words, only experience. It is there in the connection to your higher self that you gain the stuff of clarity. It comes to you pure, uncontaminated by particulars of any kind. And to receive it, you must let go of those very particulars that are clouded by confusion, angst, disturbances.

Greet your own pure existence as it was created to be and simply melt into it until its time to continue on in your life freshly endowed with all you need. Here lies the great mystery that you can know, but not explain, even to yourself.

What you can do is to live from that knowing. It is your lifeboat.

Self-judgement is only an element of general judgement. Humans sort out the diversity of experience, other humans, and all the vast elements of human life through an intricate system of assessments or conclusions. Good and bad and countless shades of each comprise our strategy for navigating through life with all its complexities. A strategy is needed, but often it is formed by responses to individual experiences, family, associations with others, culture, and religion, to name a few.

But what is the foundation of our judgements? Self-judgement is almost entirely based on how others respond to us. But most others are as confused as we are. So, what is the level of accuracy of these judgements that have such an imposing influence on our lives?

When it comes to the judgement of where we are in consciousness, we are not the ones who are able to judge—not that that stops us. We don't have the perspective in and of ourselves to see the whole journey, or even, in some cases, what is better or worse. But we can rightly assume that the judgements we characteristically make are inaccurate and based on a major lack of perspective.

True observation is judgement free. Hence, it has the capacity to see what is without obstruction. From observation comes knowing, not *about* but of that which is observed. Once capsulized dutifully by our limited brains, the knowing fades within the restrictions of our capacity. Essential knowing is not limited, cannot be described, and disappears if we judge it.

The human dilemma. The ability to judge is an essential survival tool. Should you cross that street, touch that plant, eat that food, or trust that person? You need this ability to survive and thrive. But people also misuse it to shrink their world to an understandable, possibly controllable, size.

Like any tool, judgment needs to be used carefully and respected as a weapon with the capacity to do great harm.

The happenings are all being united, coming to a focal point. Everything is about one thing. You don't have to understand that, just know it. Human beings are experts at dividing things up—work and play, love, and hate, good and bad. All of them are part of the coming together that is underway. All that you are, all that you do, is part of where your life is going, where life itself is going, from the perspective of infinity, of timeless time.

At times the experience is intense, all consuming, but there is a rhythm to it. There is intensity and peacefulness, the sublime and the raucous, the forceful and the gentle, the serious and the light. So, diversion is not what you seek—just the natural flow of the evolution. You may not have any idea what this means in the sense that you could explain it, but you know the truth of it. Lay down the divisions and hold on to the unity of all things. You can live in that unity, that oneness. Open to that and see what you see. Enjoy the company.

The aim is not to try to be perfect; it is to appreciate perfection. You have a core desire, but many others flit around the fire. All can serve the one. Trust that it is happening even now.

You are protected, and you have a part to play. Like a blind person, feel your way. When you feel despair, when you catch yourself believing in impossibility, laugh in its face and be grateful that you noticed. Flood your space with your gratitude, for like light, it extinguishes darkness.

When there is too much to do, think what you could do joyfully. It is the way of doing rather than the what that makes the difference. The accumulated mass of all your doings is for nothing except for the quality of being you bring into each moment. It is with a loving smile that the human habit of resisting happiness is observed: "Anything but that!" until you get a mouthful of it and then it's, "More, please, more."

Everything is a gift—everything—if it is held in the knowing of infinite.

When the purpose is one-pointed, the intention pure and undiluted, such is the power that emerges. What does it take to see the gift and pick it out from the thick of darkness? Humility, openness to new ways of seeing, connection with the heart's deepest longing, enough trust to lay down the burden while holding on to the love.

Every scene in life offers the chance to see the breath of the eternal blowing through you. There is no need to understand it, but you can recognize the feeling of it—the lightness, the gracefulness, the vibrant warmth of love manifesting. Such can be yours each moment of the day. Can you accept that? Can you welcome the spirit that dwells within? From the gift of that consciousness all others flow.

*Y*ou are continually doing things in your life, moving toward goals, interacting with people, places, things. But all this that you so erroneously call your life, all this you are so busy with, is not the essence of your actual life. What you are always doing, whatever else is going on, is transmitting energy.

Step back—out of your life in time—and ask, "What kind of energy am I transmitting? Where is my consciousness affixed? Are my channels clogged or open?" For the only doing that matters is that of being, of awareness, of connectedness to the eternal flow of life energy. That is what you have the opportunity to transmit, to be in sync with, as you do all your doings.

In this realm of connection in the succeeding moments of now, there is initially no doing on your part. There is only choice, listening, reaching for the knowing that descends in a swirl of peace or exhilaration and trusting it.

Sometimes that comes naturally. Sometimes it literally takes all you have, just to hold on. Remember that when you ask for help with a willingness to accept it when it comes, it comes in abundance. All you need to do at that point is to allow the obvious actions to take place and behold, as chains are broken and freedom emerges triumphant.

Appreciate the wonder of it, of what you could never bring about on your own. Feel gratitude, recognize, and accept the gift. Know that you are playing a part in a bigger story than you can see. These are truly moments of enlightenment, where the light passes through you, lighting up the very core of your being as it does.

These high moments of recognition invigorate the fire of your longing for that state of being, that state of equilibrium, which feels at once so natural and so foreign. Make it your familiar, your normal. It is not so strange to be in the physical world and live in freedom from the forces of confusion and delusion that abound.

You have the keys to unlock the doors that shut you into your own private prison. It is up to you to use them. Tolerate no longer the ties that bind. Hold firmly, with the power of your intention, your attention, to the one tie that frees you, heals, cleanses, allows the light to shine through. That is your privilege and your joy and your destiny.

*E*very human being asks the critical question at some point or many in their life: Who am I? So often their answer is formed by the way society, friends, and family name them—child, student, mother, father—or by what they do professionally. The answer forms silently in their minds, offering both superficial comfort and limitation. It doesn't satisfy or resolve the question that merely sinks deeper within, unanswered like a hope given up on.

And why? Why is this question so universal and so essential to answer? Partly because it leads to another question. Why do I exist, here and now? What is this sometimes-crazy life all about as it maneuvers its way through all the possibilities from the mundane to the sublime?

There is a reason the question never goes away. There is a deep need to explore it and to continue finding the answers through one's life. Within each one lives a spirit, an eternal flame, an essence of being; and we need to know it, to be able to connect with it, to discover it. That energy is somehow distilled, separate from our roles, our past, our emotions and doings. It has an existence outside all that and, as such, offers us the key to joyful and meaningful survival. Some call it soul, some higher self, some atman. There are many names, many understandings, but a common thread runs through them all.

This self, this "I" that you are, is the one capable of living through many lives. It is separate from your personality with all the characteristics that you think of as you—strengths and weaknesses, likes and dislikes, looks and stages. It offers the human being of your name at this time the opportunity of climbing out of the tangle of your life into a place of apart—a place of quintessential joy where you can see differently, be filled with strength, courage, clarity—whatever you need. It is not just your lifeline but the fuel of your life.

Whether you are bored, angry, confused, frustrated, sad, or empty, it neutralizes negativity that you may be open to what you need. When you are in a positive state of excitement, enchantment, determination, purpose, and their like, you gain access to the perspective that lifts you above circumstances and allows you to sense the thread of the primal purpose that is the key to your well-being, even as such circumstances and emotions fluctuate in the winds of change.

So, above all, seek that "I," that eternal spark on its aeonic journey home through the world of separation and conflict to that of oneness with utter being. Seek your individual purpose along the way. Learn to be free of what pulls you off your course. Hold on to your connection with infinite as it manifests through you, and all that is beyond description, beyond words and names, expands your being, your seeing, your knowing. Help is there but for the asking. Strength and courage await your call. Arms of love and comfort wait to sooth your cry. Again and again and again.

Human beings live in a state of duality, within themselves and within the physical world of our planet. When the seemingly opposing elements of a duality mesh together, a transformation takes place through which they enhance each other in a benign balance, such as the force of gravity pulling an airplane down and the force of wind flow keeping it air born.

Initially, in human life the balance is fragile, easily disturbed, and held with tremendous effort by the one who seeks it. Disturbing a strong bond of balance can be catastrophic as is splitting an atom.

As individuals seeking balance at the core of conflicting desires, the challenge to hold the place of serenity becomes tougher, just as the learning of any subject matter of substance and complexity becomes more and more difficult and demanding.

Humans are the only ones who have a choice in these matters, and that makes them special among all of creation. Amidst the struggle, try to recognize the specialness and profound possibility of your state. Find gratitude for the opportunity to struggle. Value the possibility of victory, of the naturalness and the ecstasy of the coming together of opposites, and the strength and the beauty of the perfection of the result, even if temporary. Ask yourself frequently, when all seems filled with conflict, what actually matters in the long run?

Emotions are a condition of human life. Attention and intention are choices made by a human soul, even as emotions swarm. The emotions aren't bad or good. They can be doors to understanding. The choice of directed focus is powered by will and courage.

There is an essential self that just wants the freedom to be how it is.

*A*ll life is connected, but few have the eyes to see that. You see yourself as separate, defined in form by the very skin of your body. And here lies a great mystery. As a human being with consciousness, you are an individual with recognizable characteristics — totally unique DNA that partially determines your form, talents, even preferences. And at the same time, you are a microcosm within the macrocosm.

You are part of all, endowed with the gift, should you discover it and choose to accept it, of expanding your individual consciousness into that of all. It is there that you find wholeness, equilibrium. It is that consciousness that invites you to truly "dance with the stars," see everything that crosses your path in a different light.

When you raise, expand, your consciousness more and more into the whole of creation, you feel the merging, the ecstasy of love offered, received, and returned; the peace of longing fulfilled. Each time you walk again in your body on the ground beneath you, you walk differently by degrees, for you bring the light down with you, the very vibration of the source of creation.

With that comes the possibility of conquering darkness, pain, separation, illness—all that is negative and operates with the force of a vacuum, pulling substance into its void. In contrast, you have begun to receive the magnetic power of wholeness, which attracts its own back to its self.

Go often to the well to drink the water of eternal life, and then go about your life until you begin to thirst again. You are accustomed to living in the desert; it seems normal to you. Living in the light of the larger view will become your new normal in time.

Your destiny, if you accept it, is to allow the timeless to shine through you in the world of time. In that context the so-called trials of life seem small. They have no power to pull you into negativity. See them as opportunities to practice holding on to the greater view, the highest consciousness you can attain in the midst of all that could lure you away.

Choice and effort are the parents of the strength and courage you will need. Those are your tools. All else comes naturally to the one who can trust. Be that one. Be of the one.

Let the butterfly of transformation drink from the rose of love as they take wing together to evolve the souls of man and womankind.

Do you have any idea how much you color what comes before you with your emotions, opinions, automatic responses, built out of past confusions? Do you want to remove those glasses and see what is as it is? See without judgment and reactivity? Observe?

Much of what seems familiar you do not actually know. It has morphed into something else, but you do not recognize that. You haven't noticed. Remember, nothing is static.

As you steer your way through your world—the small patch of reality that you encounter in your life—make every effort you can to disentangle yourself from the "familiar" and see as though you haven't seen before. The wisdom of what you have learned will stay with you. The false will fade into the background. You will be surprised by what you will see, what you will understand, when your seeing is untainted by the past.

A streetlight shines equally for the thief and the saint. It has no choice. As one through whom the light of eternity can shine, you do have choice—the choice to let the light come through unobstructed, uncontaminated. It is not to say that familiarity with things, people, places, is not important. You need a certain accumulated knowledge to survive. What is important is to be aware of the effect of past judgments that tend to create molds for living beings who are in a constant state of change. Maybe some are becoming more hardened in certain grooves; maybe change has slowed down for them so that it is barely noticeable. But it is there.

If you want to observe truly, you don't need to forget your past experiences, but rather to move out of the judgment mode into objectivity. It's harder than you think. You may think you know from experience that a person lies easily and therefore question what he or she says. That is wise. What gets in the way of seeing the present is your personal reaction to your past experiences—the hurt, anger, jealousy, disparagement etc. That is your part in perpetuating the mold and possibly obscuring your ability to see change. You try to hold another to what you know of them and fail to see the new emerging, subtle as it may be.

When you simply become aware of this phenomenon, acknowledge that everything with form in your world from a stone to a person is evolving, you will begin to enjoy this new way of seeing. Be curious, open to the unexpected. Let yourself be surprised, and, best of all, be free of the obstacles or barriers to seeing clearly. As your projections evaporate in the sunlight, your responses will be more appropriate.

It can be lifesaving, this, or life giving, or many things in between. Truth—be it ugly or beautiful or shades of both— needs to be seen as fully as you are able. If you don't see dirt, you will not be able to remove it. If you don't see beauty, you will not appreciate it. And if you don't feel the touch of infinite presence, you will not be able to glory in it. It was not ill said that "the truth shall make you free."

*Y*our fundamental understanding of what is important shifts as you see happenings and physical states from a perspective of the eternal energy, which is one of movement and transformation.

If you focus on the immediately perceptible story of goings-on, you see a limited drama in which your personal advantage is tightly intertwined with the physical. From the perspective of the ongoing flow of creation, all that is physical and all that is not is in motion along an evolutionary path of expansion and contraction, moving from one into many and many into one.

You are essentially one of many moving into one. That is all anything is really about within the individualized drama of your life as you know it. As a human being, you are placed in the middle where you can look into the world of the physical and the world of the ethereal and experience both. You are constantly at a crossroad where you choose your way of seeing and your direction. You will look up or down, expand or contract as a result.

Along the path of your spirit to its home, the measures are less and less physical. The progress is from measurable to measureless. The concepts of amount, size, and worth are not pertinent. What you have to work with is being—becoming, moving, expanding, or opening to your potential.

As you learn to focus on a single purpose, a single path, a single direction, all that you see changes its place in your understanding. Big becomes small; significant becomes inconsequential; threat is incapacitated by protection; feeling is seated in love; and on it goes as you go along.

Your understanding of these words will come from the kind of experience that is knowable but indescribable. The knowing that comes from it will be expressed in your being, not in words. The work is one of holding, keeping steady in your light even as sadness, concern, disappointment knock upon your door or seep through the cracks. Ask to learn.

Life continues beyond the one you know. Hold on to the thread of love through the microseconds of being and give thanks. Absorb the sweetness, the melody, the weightless resonance—all the gifts—until all else is cleared away. This is the way of the I that you are, and yet it seems new to you— new and very old all at once. Let go and watch the show.

"Going" logically follows "being." You clearly are; you exist. So before considering what you are going to undertake, how about considering what state of being, of consciousness, you are in? Start with: positive or negative? How does your heart, your center of love, feel about things? Abandoned? Starved? So-so? Content?

Feed the heart by opening the door to the channel of love that it thrives on. The faucet is on, but the nozzle to the hose is shut. Turn it to open; look for the openness within yourself to the love beyond understanding. It is not hard unless you are being stubborn, avoiding what you cannot understand or control.

The truth is that it's up to you. You are the one who decides whether or not to make yourself available to what is there for you. Let the din of struggle melt in the knowing of peace, well-being, and joy. Then and only then look at the circumstances that you don't like and see them for what they are and what they are not. As you do that, their power over you diminishes. You may have "obligations" or "shoulds" awaiting you, but only you can decide how or if to approach them. Look for what your heart really wants and listen to its voice.

Go to the place where you know nothing because you are part of everything—not apart but part. Then carry that taste of everything into the fabric of all the parts, woven together in the story of your current life. That knowing, held onto, shows you the way through the tangles, and allows the miracle of being all and part at the same time. You have to let go of your grasp of both to allow them to blend.

Feed the heart by opening the door to the channel of love that it thrives on. The faucet is on, but the nozzle to the hose is shut. Turn it to open; look for the openness within yourself to the love that passes understanding. It is not hard unless you are being stubborn, avoiding what you cannot understand or control.

The doing of opening to the silence is the only doing that precedes being. That's because you have the inborn right of choice about that. The hard truth is that it's up to you. You alone decide whether to make yourself available to what is there for you. Let the din of struggle melts in the knowing of peace, well-being, and joy. Then and only then look at the circumstances that you don't like and see them for what they are and what they are not.

As you do that, their power over you diminishes. You may have "obligations" or "shoulds" awaiting you, but only you can decide how or if to approach them. Look for what your heart really wants and listen to its voice.

When you find and choose the path of trust, everything changes irrevocably. Just as the burden falls from your shoulders, so does the mistaken idea that you can control your life. Do not confuse control with responsibility. You seek control in some frantic effort to survive with a sense of security in this chaotically changing world. To achieve it, you grasp at certain elements of sameness in your relationships, surroundings, and circumstances.

Homeostasis seems to offer a certain comfort, even as you seek to improve your life—to make it more secure but also more fulfilling. These are opposing desires. One is rooted in the illusion that you have any control over the big things: over nature, other people's actions and intents, war and peace among nations, economic swings, to name a few. Needing the illusion, you grasp at the little things in your life that seem to be more within your reach. They may be, but ruling over them does not give you the control you seek.

Trust is another matter. It comes from a profound understanding. There is one thing you have been granted control over, and that is choice. You would rather not see that, right? As your life proceeds from birth, the web of involvements becomes more and more complex up to a certain point, and then it begins to simplify, like the incoming and outgoing of one huge wave. In this ocean of change that stems from forces beyond your knowing, what can you trust, and how do you trust it?

The waters get deep here. Can you swim in them? Do you have the strength and the courage to do that? In truth, is that what you want? Or do you prefer the comfort of illusion?

You have a fundamental desire. You were born with it, but not with the knowing of it. Life offers you the opportunity to discover it, and if you so choose, to fulfill it—first in gifted moments that fade and eventually in moments that flow together with growing power.

That wave, that desire, you can trust but not control. You have neither the knowledge nor the power to guide it. Infinite cannot be guided for it simply IS. Let that infinite be your North Star; let it guide you. It will only do so with your permission—that one element of choice that always remains in your hands.

This battle between illusion and trust is waged in the moments of your days, the little things that accumulate without your notice. Is this getting uncomfortable? Is your attention turning to the demands of your very busy day?

What will you reach for? The swirl of demands and activities that feature you as the star player? Or the acknowledgement that you don't necessarily know which of those activities and efforts even matter?

When you let go of the need for illusion, you see everything differently. You find an openness to the unexpected, a wisdom beyond your understanding. You find a the kind of clarity that results when the clutter of possibilities and impossibilities is blown away and peace begins to shine within and through you.

Along the Way

Seek first the trustworthy, and what you need the most, want the most, will find its way naturally to you. That is inevitable, and it is your choice—a huge one made in tiny moments.

So how do you do that, you ask. How do you find your way through the tiny moments toward your primary goal, once you have become aware of it? How?

It is a matter of awareness, of remembering. When you get immersed in whatever circumstances you are involved in— whether they be struggles or pleasures, mundane routine, or a challenging effort— remember. Keep an ear open. It's called staying in the present, even as you look forward. Since childhood you were trained to look for cars when you cross a street, even as you are thinking about where you are going or why. That is for your safety.

So, when you are walking through your life, be alert as well— not just for signs of danger but for possibility. Listen for the voice of your greater knowing, the one you come by when you are in silent contact with your higher self. That is the source of knowing that enables you to see differently, to keep in touch with the source of understanding within you.

The key is effort. It is effort that unlocks the door, opens the way. Simple. So simple, yet out of reach for most. Focus on the effort, not the failure. Think of a babe learning to walk. Be propelled by that instinctive need to walk and just keep at it with the singularity of the little one that has no thought to judge its failure, just delights in its progress. A loving hand is ever there to catch you...

You can only go forward from where you are, and frankly, you are not a good judge of that. All your opinions about yourself and others are just that—opinions. They can cloud your sight, your ability to observe.

Set your intention in the morning before the day of action begins and stay tuned to it. Go forward as an observer, allowing yourself the widest view of what is before you. It can be exhilarating and so very freeing.

Go to the place where you know nothing because you are part of everything—not apart but part. Then carry that taste of everything into the fabric of all the parts, woven together in the story of your current life. That knowing, held onto, shows you the way through the tangles, allows the miracle of being all and part at the same time. You have to let go of your grasp of both to allow them to blend. The other parts are also the whole.

In the realm of all that IS, all the opposites that humans perceive and are thrown around by are actually in perfect balance—a state of neutrality in which the consciousness of the one who can open to it expands in bliss until it is time to return to the life he or she is living in the world of time.

As you reach for that balance in your life, you find a viewpoint that is not tangled by disturbances and allows you to see more clearly what simply is. No threat or excitement. And in the light of that clarity, choices, options, and pathways become obvious and simple, although not always immediately.

Making the effort to step out of your own entanglements is the first choice, oft to be repeated until the flow becomes the natural state. It is after all, the natural state. The price is simple: letting go of control. The reward is the very safety we so valiantly seek through control.

If you don't like what you see going on around and within you and you see no action to change it, a common strategy is to simply put up a wall, so you are spared seeing it. Nothing changes except your constant reminder of the situations you don't like.

An alternative would be to look at the disturbing thing from a different perspective. From an airplane, the tallest building is but a dot on the landscape, the Chinese Wall but a curving line without apparent height. So, what is this perspective but the larger view? The shift reveals your own freedom, the mobility of spirit that is not dependent on circumstances.

As your attention goes where that spirit lives, the very within of your being, you are no longer endangered by the situations that seem so dark. The perception of danger or of being trapped dissolves and no longer needs to be hidden by your walls or diversions. In the moment of now, time recedes, and the fullness of well-being expands.

Loss carves out space for the new. Some fill it with sorrow, which becomes a new identity. Some find a way to keep it open and clean, like an empty drawer, until a new gift can settle there, a new understanding. Losses can destroy, corrode the spirit, or strengthen it by demonstrating or bringing into view that which is not touched by it.

We learn early that we have needs—those related to survival but also the need for love, connection with others, enjoyment, and more. What cannot be learned but only discovered is that which cannot be adequately named but which is constant, the ultimate fulfiller of all needs.

Along the Way

Ah, the discovery! It is seemingly an endless process that dissolves in the timelessness of the infinite. Who but a human amongst the creatures of Earth can approach it? That ability is the first gift, and it lies hidden in many. The next gift is to touch upon it, "accidentally" or with effort. A pathway opens inviting the person to walk upon it in trust.

The pathway can be twisted and obscured by obstacles, difficulties, diversions, and false images. It is also littered with pots of treasure, each offering the strength and courage to go on in response to the feeblest, but sincere, effort.

As each treasure or new gift is discovered, the innate response of longing, gratitude, and joy is awakened, renewed. The nature of the emotion of feeling loss to gravitate to similar feelings and experiences from both the recent and distant past, thus forming a larger, less identifiable mass. That's why it is helpful and wise to present each incident of feeling loss to the light of your understanding. See it clearly and find its gift to you—a gift of revealing the ropes that bind you so that you may loosen them and let the feeling dissolve,

The human way of looking at the events in their lives is to evaluate them as good or bad, happy, or sad, advantageous or disadvantageous, and so on. The perspective from above is entirely different.

So many happenings that occur on the stage of your life's play are potentially bridges for you to progress into a higher consciousness. As a matter of fact, any happening, situation, condition, or other person can be such. The choice is yours.

You are the one who gives power to what lies outside of you. Do you see that? As you recognize a challenge or a delight, you have the option of seeing it in the context of the light—the ever-moving energy of the source of all seeking to engage human kind.

Some things that go on in and around you in your life make you sad; some make you happy, angry, or amazed. The emotions are not the problem in themselves. The overarching feeling of love has room for them all. It has the power to transform the small and the petty, the constricting and the undermining, into the splendor of glimpsing the possibility each moment offers you.

Can you walk across the bridge from hurt into love? From anger into love? From fear into love? From passion into love? Is that what you want to do? It is a learning that opens from your true desire. When you are caught up in a circumstance— positive or negative—ask for the learning, and you will be given the key to walk across the bridge into a more profound way of seeing, into an awareness that sets you free from bondage of any kind.

So, when earth life gets a hold of you, ask to learn, make the effort to see as from above, to open to the very light of life, the all-encompassing love that waits to embrace you and yours. Yield to that and discover who and what you are.

*A*s we grow in life, we develop a variety of tendencies, a personality unique to each one. Some of these tendencies may be self-destructive and others productive. The former block our way to intended goals. The latter opens doors to creativity, insights, and unique gifts to offer others.

So as individuals living with qualities that obstruct and those that flow, do we become stagnant? Stuck? We have choices, but only when we recognize the source of the stagnancy. Only when we begin to understand the power of free choice.

The first step is to recognize the block to the freedom we seek. These blocks may be so familiar that they remain disguised and hidden from view. Recognition is the first step in making a choice, to become free of the trigger reactions of fear, ambition, pride, self-doubt, lack of trust, the need to be thought well of, etc.

One must see the aberration to let go of it, often repetitively. Recognize it as the obstacle it is to the very things, we want the most, long for the most—the place of pure heart and the mind that embraces it—love and wisdom as one.

So, first recognition, then choice, then courage, then the freedom to grow strong, to fulfill one's inborn potential, to fly. In a lifetime, there are obstacles and potential breakthroughs. Growing pains?

What steers one through the inner wars? The light of the longing for freedom, love, and evolution. Fear vs. Love: which one will win the case of our life? The jury is out; the judge is patient. What is unique is that the one on trial, so to speak, still has the power of choice, the chance to quell the warring factors again and again until the weapons are dropped, and the war is dissolved. In the battles of old, the General climbs the mountain to get a full perspective of the battle. In the battles within, we are the General and the mountain top is the place of peace within. Doubt and fear are generally related to something specific. Love and knowing are unrestricted. Live in open wonder.

Oh, what it is to be a human being! Obstacles and openings, all within a single human soul. Living beings of all levels eat for strength and eliminate for cleansing. The human being is no exception on a basic level, but the human being has some say about what to take in and what to let go of, and that makes all the difference.

*Y*ou cannot walk upon the path of another, though you constantly compare yours to that of others. It is fantasy. Your road is yours alone, even as you weave through the traffic of others, both known and unknown, seen and unseen. It is keeping your eye on your own road that will save you from many a useless complication.

Understand the difference between involvement and entanglement. You live in a world of groups, many overlapping. You interact with many people, are drawn to or repelled by some, merely pass others by. It all has purpose, but as certain emotions come in, you lose sight of what that purpose might be.

Love is not embracing all that another is and does. Sometimes it is merely seeing the beauty that may be covered over so that the other may see or feel it as well. If they do, what they do about it is their choice. Holding your own is not selfish, though it is certainly of the self. It is the only state from which you can truly give to someone else.

Think about a light bulb. To shed light on the area around it, it must be turned on. Its filaments need to be connected with a source of power. Then when its light flows outward according to its strength, it does not direct that light, nor does it have a say in who shall receive it or for what purpose.

You who have free choice and a whole set of ideas, mostly skewed, about what should and shouldn't be, could learn something from that inanimate light bulb. Be the channel, not the source of power. Your work is not to decide where light is needed or what it should do but to keep yourself connected to your higher self, free of the negative emotions that roll in around you and block clear insight. Get out of the way.

Even as you take care of responsibilities, you can be on vacation from the internal struggles generated by the masses of beings on this planet, each with their own objectives, concerns, and desires. What is your desire? In its simplest form, that desire at the core of your very life will set you free. It is essentially all that matters, and it holds the key to all the so-called "issues" that loom around you, bringing nothing but confusion if allowed to come between you and your place of knowing.

Let go the heaviness, for it is not yours to carry. Look carefully at what you have trouble letting go of, at what undermines your trust. Look again at what seems impossible, too dire a possibility to face. These are truly the elements of illusion.

You have the tools to open locked doors; you have the courage to hold on to chosen purpose. The rest is a matter of being an observer. Watch the play even as you are in it. Play your part with a light heart, a heart of light. Then whatever needs to be will be.

*D*eep in the farthest reaches of existence, and even in the nearest, lies utter perfection. It only requires recognition for its manifestation—recognition and appreciation, gratitude. Strangely enough, all the imperfections require the same qualities—recognition and gratitude. The recognition is to see them for what they are, products of negativity. The gratitude is for the clarity that comes from the recognition.

However, the results of recognizing perfection as compared to recognizing imperfection are opposite. Recognizing perfection brings the opportunity to engage with it, let it into your being, your consciousness. Recognizing imperfection brings the opportunity to disengage.

In this process the power of perfection is increased, while the power of imperfection disintegrates. Integration versus disintegration. That is the creation and the destruction inherent in the evolution of life, of all creation.

As you observe the flashes of personality-based ego and remain in the mode of observation instead of judgment, the experience of the oneness fills all the spaces and engulfs your being. "There" becomes "here" in the eternal now.

As you observe the flashes of personality-based ego and remain in the mode of observation instead of judgment, the experience of the oneness fills all the spaces and engulfs your being. "There" becomes "here" in the eternal now.

All that is "here" joins all that is "there", wordless being simply is.

The knowing of the whole yields no precepts, no organizing principles, no right way, or wrong way, no good and no bad. Just unity, oneness, spilling its all-encompassing beauty into the multiplicity of its manifestation of which each human, each atom, is a part. Outside of time, the wholeness absorbs diversity even as diversity still exists. And there is no contradiction here.

Now and forever, love and hate, good and evil, yin and yang are joined even as they push against each other. Although the human brain cannot comprehend this reality, it has the capacity to experience it and to be guided by the knowing of it.

The experience of the whole changes the individual's perception of what matters and thereby changes everything until that indefinable experience is allowed to recede, to be woven into an explanation where it is reduced to the manageable. It is along the seam of balance, the horizon line, between the particular and the whole that the individual can thrive.

That is, in fact, what a human being is—a being with the inherent possibility of integrating the one and the many in this world of matter and spirit in the midst of constant change. You are a part of the whole and yet still separate, able to observe the emerging reality. Open to the transformation, welcome it, and observe the mountains of obstruction dissolve.

Open to the understanding of this evolution and what it means for the remaining moments of this lifetime. In apparently losing yourself, you become your self in the world of time. Dissolve and evolve. The smallest steps have explosive power. It is up to you to take them.

When the silence sings, the melody washes away the wounds of life with the healing waters of IS. Oh, to be open to the song of all.

That which would shut out light draws lines of division between sources of light. The lines are ego-based and easily come between potential light bearers. What is so insidious and even dangerous is that ego is quite often buried inside the cloak of righteousness.

Such a challenge it is to see the light of right without grasping for possession of it—an act that ultimately destroys the very power it seeks to grasp. Light cannot be contained. Its energy is born of original source. While it can be recognized by human beings, minute particles of the whole, it cannot be grasped. The one who thinks they have done so is suffering from the ultimate illusion.

What do you want? To be right or to be an instrument of light? Don't be fooled by your own desires to be more than you are or your fear to actualize what you truly are. The unique abilities of each being of soul, developed over lifetimes of choices and learning, are a serious responsibility. Not to be taken lightly! Ha, ha!

When you focus on the light in each other, the lines of division evaporate. Therein lies the power of pure intent. Observe the blocks in another only long enough to be wise, but give your attention to that which needs to grow. Give it your attention, acceptance, and gratitude.

When we are in some form of emotional or physical crisis, our tendency is to shut down, circle the wagons, so to speak, in search of protection. That is a natural instinct that has some positive purpose. However, in the process, we are apt to shut out the very source of our healing, our own inborn connection to well-being. We shut down our knowing and seek the knowing of others.

In times of perceived threat, emotional or physical pain, turmoil, confusion, fear etc., what we need most of all is openness. Even as we feel desperate for control, life circumstances call for us to let go of fear and judgment, reactiveness, and the desire to change, fix, or escape the present moment. It is within the present moment only that we can heal, understand, know, be free of restricting definitions. Now in this smallest increment of time, is our own door to the timeless—that realm of conscious awareness of ultimate well-being.

It is through the knowing that is revealed in the delicate state of balance between opposing forces of any duality that we discover truth to the degree we are capable of embracing it. Transformation evolves naturally, ever challenging us to embrace it without reserve.

This does not mean ignoring a wrong, taking no action, squashing our own emotions or opinions. It means disengaging enough to observe the situation with some objectivity, see our options just as if we are reading a story with which we have no personal involvement.

Why do we limit our possibility? What is the fear that causes us to draw back from it? It is multifaceted and individual, but it is rooted in the perceived need for control. The paradox is that as we try so hard to control what we cannot control, we become controlled by that very need and lose our capacity for knowing the often hidden well-being of ourselves and others.

We surrender to reactivity, to the relentless conditioning of our life experience, like dogs in a Pavlovian experiment. Why be the dog? As a human being you have the capacity to choose your own intention, chart your own course.

Your actions need not be reactive ones but rather intentional connection, attention, and receptivity to the energy of spirit that is in constant readiness to work with you. New doors open as your own spirit begins to recognize its connection to the essential oneness of all.

Do you see the importance of this? In this little life in this micromoment of time, you can be a conduit to timeless, to infinite. That is when we recognize that what we deem to be magical or miraculous is actually normal, when we are in a position to watch threats dissolve, sickness yield to wellness, tiredness to vitality, frustration to attainment. We experience the cadence and power of what can be, not just in our own sphere of action but in the whole of what lies beyond our conscious awareness.

In the attempt to control what we are not wired to control, we develop a deep-seated belief in limitation instead of possibility. Moving out of that self-set limitation takes work—recognition, effort, and will along with a simple request, openness to the unknown known. All is energy. To what end do you want to spend yours?

When you experience emerging consciousness in your meditation, bring it down into the core of your very being dwelling now in this temporary physical body. Cradle it and let it cradle you. Let it expand naturally into your life as you live it. Know that the profound can express itself anytime, with or without your knowing.

Set no limits for it with your limited brain. The light of divine consciousness is infinite. Can you allow it freedom in your life? Do you have the openness, the courage, the desire to do that? You have the opportunity. It takes allowing on your part, not managing, or even understanding. It takes the strength and will to simply hold the space, hold in the space.

The state of balance that evolves is one of precise equilibrium. It is tipped neither to the negative nor to the positive. It is judgment free, reaction free—the essential condition for clear observation. You know when you are in it, for it is unmistakable. Unfortunately, you don't always know when you are not, for that knowing depends on the very consciousness you let slip quietly away.

So, keep at it and learn as you go. Find your own naturalness of being as only you can know it. Allow yourself to be useful as only you can be, as a purposefully designed thread in the tapestry of creation. This is all you can be—just what you are, all of what you are. It is no less than infinite love that waits for you to open to it, that it may shine through you and each one that has come to know of it, recognize it, feel it.

By degrees, you discover how to be in relation with the affairs of your earth life without moving away from your eternal life. It is never away from you, after all, by its very nature, its inherent definition. Know that and remember what you know.

You may not walk around in the ecstasy of your most connected moments when you are drawn in and gathered up to disappear into the beyond. For that you need to be somewhat disconnected from all that changes. Even so, the transformation continues, the evolution continues as long as you ask for it, as long as you desire it.

Hence your becoming is your being and your being is your becoming. All is well in the larger scheme of things, however it looks in the world of time. Know that and accept what you know. It is enough.

You can be there in the timeless again and again until your "agains" slip into your always.

There is almost always something to do, but we forget that at the same time there is always something to be. That being that we bring to our doing is what makes all the difference. It has the power to transform the doing, to take it into the world of experiencing the flow of life in its profound beauty. It provides a place from which to observe as opposed to becoming tangled, to create instead of resist, and to feel joy as opposed to boredom. Why do we prioritize the doing? Why let it be the ordering factor in your life while the very source of your life awaits inclusion?

You can be filled with the essence of your being as you carry out your doing. The reverse can be problematic. It takes trust to give precedence to the being part, to recognize its power to transform—a power you do not control, and that can be a challenge in itself. But it is also part of the beauty, the joy of the unexpected that you alone could never bring about.

As you give up trying to control what happens, fear of what might happen, and strain to avoid what you see as bad, you move into a new dimension. So-called problems give you practice. And as with most things, practice makes perfect or at least makes a step in that direction.

As you immerse yourself in "have to's," you resist and isolate yourself. You forget that you are loved even so. This kind of love is not withdrawn when you make mistakes, forget it, or even turn away. It can't, by its very nature. Your experience with others makes that hard to believe, but then you also don't notice your part in the separation.

You are loved as you are. Can you love others as they are? The heart that is recognized and relied upon does not need protection because it always has the love that has no limit or reason. That love follows its nature and urges you to follow yours.

Appreciate the infinity of an instant. Instants naturally flow together, only limited in this life by continuing breath. As you appreciate them, they reveal themselves as passages to your own evolution. Give them precedence over all the "goings on" and the feelings they evoke, and you will begin to recognize your capacity for joy and the unimagined gifts it offers.

The joy of recognition finds its way through all the difficulties that a human life presents. Joy reduces them to gentle speed bumps. It just needs to be allowed to exist, to be free, and to be recognized. It awaits your recognition and your attention, patiently.

Are you curious?

*I*n times of desperation, when all seems threatened, the hole of hopelessness can be filled with the power of spirit like at no other time. It is a gift. Can you grasp that? Let gratitude open your heart in trust. Be absorbed by that power. All will be as it is meant to be, for that is what is meant to be.

When you see wrong on the part of others, stay in the place of observation. Name it, if you want, but stay back from it emotionally. This is a tough order when the wrong affects you or those you love, but it is essential. Otherwise, the cluster of negativity and confusion that produced the wrong is given an entry to your own sanctuary. Before long, it owns a part of you, like a germ you pick up takes hold within your body and sickens you just when you need all your strength.

When you go beyond observation, even in your disapproval, you are giving credence to the power of the wrongdoer over you, to its ability to do you harm. This is the time when you need to stand in your own power, the power of the oneness from which you emerged. Your connection with spirit is your vehicle for finding your own answers, how to respond, if to respond. That is where you find your safety, your protection, your purpose, and your impenetrable joy.

You may feel weak, but that which can flow through you is strong. You find yourself in difficult straits—unable to see how anything will work out, caught in the perception of impossibilities. That is the time to step back. Which do you trust the most? The force of evil in all its guises or the power of the very generator of life? Let love be your shield, be it tough or gentle. Let your deepest inner knowing lead you through the tangle and watch the complications dissolve.

These are the times when everything matters when you cannot afford diversion from your course. Be alert. Listen. Trust. That which you cannot imagine waits to work with you in serving a greater purpose.

Fear and false imagining corrupts your ability to see clearly, to know what steps to take moment by moment, to spot the opportunity to move forward when it shows up. Fear welcomes in its companions— anger, jealousy, hatred, judgment, need for revenge.

You will find your strength in disentangled solitude in the seat of your own spirit calling for help and knowing without doubt that it will come. You can cry out from the place of fear, and that is wise when that is where you are. Better yet, is to circumvent fear and call out from the knowing that what you don't know is known and that you will come to know when you need to. You will find your own knowing, your own certainty. Wait, and you will find your answers. Your understanding will grow, your view will expand, and the priorities will become obvious. They are, after all, unchanging.

Learn to feel with the sensitive hands of the blind fingering the shapes of braille. See what you have never seen before, unobstructed by expectation. Listen for the distant call as it comes nearer and nearer to your straining ears in words of a language you have never been taught but know.

Even then, when you come to the point of clarity, you have the honor and dignity of choice. That is the difference between the force of evil and power of spirit. Force commands and coerces, seeks ownership of its prey, demeans its subjects. The power of spirit flows through the one who opens to it, joining together in a motion of ongoing transformation.

Epilogue

The newness of each moment is hidden by the way it flows from the previous moment to the next. Adding to that, we tend to carry the load of past moments or even large clusters of them along with us to the extent that the newness is easily missed. We ourselves change as time streams by, but do we see that change? Are we present enough to notice? To appreciate?

A survival skill of the human species is to keep looking forward in anticipation of what might happen on the road ahead. We look for the panther that might be hiding in the bushes and project our thoughts toward readiness for defense. This skill has its value, but it also pulls us away from what is really happening as opposed to what might.

The opportunity lies in awareness, the consciousness of the newness that can free one from the bindings of the past. Awareness offers the possibility of freedom from conditioning and the gift of seeing the familiar freshly. Boredom fades and the routine can be seen as new and even unpredictable, the mundane enjoyable.

It can be disturbing to be unable to look far into the future and predict the turns in life. The fact is that we cannot predict how even the most carefully planned future will turn out. Planning is fine if we remember that.

Life is for the living, and "living" implies more than continued breath. It means being there for all that is, absorbing the joy of simply being alive, of the freshness of moments attended to. Should real danger occur, the habit of being aware supports a readiness for self-protection and that of others. Try it out in short periods of time and learn, freshly. You will be amazed.

Whatever the intention, the essential self of each one is constantly changing. The person you will be at the time of anticipating an event is not the same as the one you will be should it happen, nor will it be exactly as you expected.

Presence in the present is the present. And the present is the ability to experience the constant presence of spirit, our own or that of the larger form of existence in its purest state, its eternal state.

www.ingramcontent.com/pod-product-compliance
Lightning Source LLC
LaVergne TN
LVHW041700070526
838199LV00045B/1139